FORERUNNER
MEDITATIONS

VOLUME ONE

FORERUNNER
MEDITATIONS

A SIX MONTH DEVOTIONAL FROM THE INTERNATIONAL HOUSE OF PRAYER, KANSAS CITY

VOLUME I

Edited by JOSHUA FARMER

Forerunner Meditations, Volume One
Copyright © 2004 by *The Children's Legacy*

Cover Graphics by Tom Morse-Brown

Edited by Joshua Farmer

Most Scripture quotations are from:
New King James Version (NKJV)
Copyright © 1979, 1980, 1982, by Thomas Nelson, Inc., publishers. Used by permission. All rights reserved.

Also quoted:
New American Standard Bible (NASB)
Copyright © 1960, 1962, 1963, 1968, 1971, 1972, 1973, 1975, 1977 by the Lockman Foundation. Used by permission. All rights reserved.

Holy Bible: New International Version (NIV)
Copyright © 1973, 1978, 1984, International Bible Society. Used by permission of Zondervan Publishing House. All rights reserved.

The *King James Version (KJV)*

ISBN: 1-931600-74-0

Library of Congress Cataloging-in-Publication Data:

Library of Congress Control Number 2004114701

Printed in the United States of America

Acknowledgments

The Children's Legacy would like to recognize the many who have helped with putting volume one of *Forerunner Meditations* together. To those, we say thank you! We would especially like to recognize Esther Greaves, Josh Farmer, Tom Morse-Brown and Britt Frank. Without your efforts this devotional could not have been published.

We have enjoyed the opportunity to compile and publish *Forerunner Meditations* in partnership with the IHOP-KC community. You are among some of God's best. And thanks, Mike!

We believe many of the truths brought forth in these meditations are current messages to prepare the way of the Lord. Our desire and sincere prayer is that God will reveal His heart to yours; may our marvelous Lord draw you closer to Himself!

Charles and Jane Koth
Directors of The Children's Legacy

Dedication

I want to dedicate this book to my sweet husband, Chuck Koth. Thank you for all the countless hours of fasting and prayer for our family. You have been faithful to pray for us; and it has been this sacrifice that has not just kept our children serving the Lord, but caused them to be passionate in their service.

I know that you would never have dreamed we would be changing diapers again in our fifties (for our tenth child!), but you have handled the new additions to our family with such love and pride that you'd think you were a first-time papa. I love you and I am excited that we have all eternity together!

Jane

The Koth Family

CONTENTS

CHAPTER I

Introduction to the Song of Songs

Mike Bickle

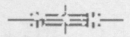

Mike Bickle is the Director of the International House of Prayer *in Kansas City, Missouri, a 24-hour-a-day ministry of "Worship with Intercession" in the spirit of the Tabernacle of David. Since September 19th, 1999, they have continued in non-stop intercession with worship and fasting teams. Currently, over 400 people serve on the full-time IHOP-KC staff in intercession, worship and fasting as they are being equipped to fulfill the* Great Commission *by reaching out in evangelism, prophetic ministry, healing the sick and providing for the poor.*

Mike is President of the Forerunner School of Ministry (FSM), *a full-time Bible school in Kansas City. The vision of FSM is, in the context of divine encounter, enjoyable prayer and transcendent worship, to thoroughly train forerunners in the knowledge of God for mighty and extravagant expressions of love. Mike has also authored* Passion for Jesus, Growing in the Prophetic, The Pleasures of Loving God, *and* After God's Own Heart. *Mike's teaching emphasizes how to grow in passion for Jesus through intimacy with God.*

For more information on the International House of Prayer *in Kansas City (IHOP-KC), the* Forerunner School of Ministry (FSM), *or upcoming conferences and events, please visit* www.fotb.com.

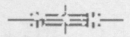

Day 1 – Introduction to the Song of Songs

There are many different ways of interpreting the Song of Songs (also called Song of Solomon), but the message of love is undeniably the key focus. From Genesis to Revelation, the Bible proclaims the love of God for His people, but no other book expresses this truth as uniquely as the Song of Songs. The actual concept that God's heart is ravished over us is not unique, but the way that it is expressed in this individual book is unparalleled. Certain aspects of our heart can only be touched through divine poetic romance. Divine romantic language touches a deep part of our being in ways that other aspects of God's truth do not.

In the same way that our eyes respond best to light and our ears respond best to sound, our hearts respond best to this concentrated revelation of His passion. Other parts of our human makeup respond to other benefits, which are wonderful foundational doctrines we never outgrow.

God wants to touch the entirety of your heart. Jesus said, "You shall love the Lord God with your whole heart (Matt. 22:37)." The heart is like a diamond with many different angles and facets. God doesn't want to touch one part of our heart, He wants to fascinate and engage our whole heart.

The reality that the beautiful Man Christ Jesus is ravished over His Bride is displayed so intimately through the Song of Songs. When you begin to understand, it will take your heart to a whole new level. When you begin to comprehend the way God feels about you, the way you feel about Him will be completely transformed. The depth of His love is unlimited; His whole heart is set on us. When this truth becomes reality, you cannot help but love Him with your whole heart in return.

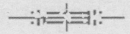

Prayer: I believe that You are a God full of emotions and passionate desires for me as Your eternal Bride. I accept this truth about who You are. Your heart is overflowing with emotions and longings for me! Pour out more truth about Your heart and emotions towards me. Let this truth open up my soul, that I might know You more intimately. Give me insight into Your heart through the Song of Songs, for I long to know You more.

Day 2 – Meditation Principles

In Scripture, I define two broad categories of truth related to meditation. First, there are truths that exhort us *to believe* God's Word, and second, there are truths that exhort us *to obey* God's Word.

Today, we will focus on how to respond to the truth exhorting us *to obey* God's Word. For example, the Lord exhorts the Bride to arise in obedience to follow Him to the mountains of hardship and risk, leaving the comfort zone (Song 2:8-10). The Holy Spirit also exhorts us to obey truths like this. He is calling His Beloved to leave everything behind in order to follow Him.

As you read through the Songs of Songs, *commit yourself to obey Jesus*, specifically in the way described in the particular passage you are reading. Speak to Jesus the intent of your heart to obey the passage and set your heart to follow through. Make small, sweet resolutions to obey Him in a specific way, and it will strengthen your obedience over time. He is committed to helping you do what He asks you to do. So commit your heart to obey Him, and He will give you grace to follow through.

Ask the Lord to *empower your heart to obey a particular truth*. Such requests for divine aid to obey will result in a growth in grace over time.

In the passage where Jesus exhorts us to arise in obedience and follow Him to the mountains of hardship and risk, stop and say, "I commit myself to obey the challenge You have set before me." Then take the next step and say, "Empower me by Your Spirit to obey this truth set before me." As you read the scriptures throughout this book, ask the Lord to teach you to commit and obey.

Prayer: *Father of all goodness, come and empower my heart to obey Your call to rise up and come away with You. Teach me to incline my ear to hear the voice of my Bridegroom calling and respond to the sweetness of His words. Empower my heart to obey You and all of Your ways, so that I might grow in the fullness that You have for my life.*

Day 3 – Initial Longing for Love and the Unlocking of Your Heart, Part 1

Song of Songs 1:2

Let Him kiss me with the kisses of his mouth for Your love is more delightful than wine.

This is a deep cry for the divine kiss—a longing for more revelation of the Bridegroom's love towards His Bride. It is not a literal kiss on the mouth; it is simply a metaphor speaking of the deepest things that God gives to the human spirit. This scripture represents the chief desire of every Believer, which is the longing for more of God.

This specific kiss represents the Holy Spirit working through the Word to enlarge our capacity to receive the affections of God. It is the first step into true intimacy because it is the request for pure, unfaltering love to be released in order for us to walk fully in intimacy with the Son of God. We were created to live eternally as the Bride of Christ, so when our hearts begin to accept this truth, we cannot help but long for more of our Lover, the Lord Jesus Christ.

The *Bridal Paradigm*, the understanding of the intense, passionate love relationship between Christ and the Christian, is necessary if we are to receive the most benefit from this Song. It is the beginning of our journey to restore the First Commandment in our lives. It starts with the longing to be fascinated by the beauty and love of Christ more than the things this world has to offer. This is the desire our hearts have when we have tasted the goodness of God; we cannot help but cry for the kisses of His Word being made manifest in our lives. Allow yourself to cry out for more revelation, because without understanding, your heart will never reach its fullest potential: to pursue Him wholly.

Prayer: *Father, would You let Your Son come and kiss my heart with the kisses of His Word. I desire nothing besides Him, and I long to know Him more. Send the Holy Spirit to enlarge my capacity to receive all that You will give to my heart. Give me a deeper desire for more of Your Son, that I might love Him more.*

Day 4 – The Initial Longing for Love and the Unlocking of Your Heart, Part 2

The journey begins with your longing for a kiss, and it will end with the seal of fiery love upon your heart, a supernatural love that many waters cannot quench (Song of Songs 8:6). This, however, is a very specific request, and not a general one. It is asking for a specific aspect of God's grace to be poured upon your life in order for your heart to be awakened to pursue Him more fully. The wonderful part is that it starts as a request, but it will eventually end as a seal.

There is a three-fold anointing of the divine kiss: the anointing to perceive (Eph. 1:17), the anointing of love (Eph. 3:6), and the anointing to make known or communicate with power (Eph. 3:8). When the Holy Spirit reveals the Bridal Paradigm to you (the Bride and Bridegroom relationship seen throughout Scripture), your heart will begin to be unlocked and you will find yourself being wooed by the romance of the Gospel, rightly called "the Divine love letter." Viewing the Bible as a romance enables the Believer to live in another realm of understanding. The request is to "unlock my heart specifically to the revelations of the beauty of the Bridegroom and the Bride," and results in the romance of the Gospel as the ideal context to best fulfill the commandments and the Great Commission.

As you continue with these devotionals, ask God to kiss you with understanding and revelation. Ask Him that through the kiss of His love, your heart might be unlocked to the fullness of His love and your spirit would be energized to pursue Him in a greater way. Ask Him to increase longing deep inside your heart that you may continue to ask for the divine kiss. Eventually, as you continue to seek intimacy and love, your heart cannot help but be awakened with desire as He places His seal on your heart.

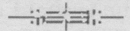

Prayer: *Awaken my heart fully to pursue love and intimacy with You. I want the kisses of Your Word so that I might have the fullness of love. Strengthen my spirit to seek after You and You alone, for nothing in this world can compare to Your beauty. Unlock the deepest places of my heart, and grant my request for more revelation of the Bridegroom and Bride.*

Day 5 – God's Drawing Us Into Intimacy and Partnership

Song of Songs 1:4

Draw me away! ...We will run after You.

This is the next key step in the journey for more of God. First, the cry is for more revelation and an unlocking of the heart. Now the cry is for more revelation and for the drawing away of your heart. It is asking to be brought into a secret place of intimacy with God, away where He is. It is a longing to be an extravagant worshipper of God and a partner in ministry with Jesus. The running represents the obedience of a heart longing just to be near the will of God.

May you open up the secret places of your heart to deep searching of the Holy Spirit, who exposes all things that you might grow up into Him who is the Head (Ephesians 1:22-23). This will require long and loving meditation on this portion of Scripture with an open and honest heart before God. Pray that He will draw you after Himself until you are made fully willing to run with Him into utter obedience. Ask the Lord to draw you near, in order to strengthen the responses of your heart towards Him. The closer you are to His heart, the more you will understand what He is thinking and what He is feeling. This empowerment of truth about His heart will encourage your inner man to fully obey His biddings. The very fact that you long to be called closer ravishes His heart in ways that not even the angels can.

Prayer: Abba, draw me after Yourself. Pursue my heart and do not stop until I am fully willing to obey and leave everything behind to follow You. Call me closer to where You are through the Scripture, and in that place bring me near to You that I might fully obey Your direction.

Day 6 – Even in My Weakness, I Am Lovely

Song of Songs 1:5

I am dark, but lovely, oh daughters of Jerusalem, like the tents of Kedar, like the curtains of Solomon.

This confession of faith amidst struggle reveals a very important truth that enables you to grow in holy passion. In order for you to consistently grow spiritually, it requires that you know you are lovely to God even while you are in the process of discovering the darkness of your heart.

Many times Christians disqualify themselves from receiving gifts from God. They allow their sins and weakness to lead their decisions and define who they are. The idea that our sins characterize who we are is such a contradiction compared to who God says we are. If you have become born again in Christ Jesus, then He has taken your sins to the grave, never to be remembered. You are now a co-heir with Christ, and as His Bride, you are one with His flesh. Therefore, your weakness or sin is not what defines who you are; the light of His countenance living inside you defines who you are.

Another common theory is that if God found out how truly sinful you are, He could not possibly want you. *How is He going to react when He discovers the sinfulness of my heart?* Many people feel overpowered by their sin, and it causes them to run *from* God instead of *to* God. In reality, if you are dirty, you need to run back to the open arms of the One who died to make you clean. When you try to hide your sin and run away from God, you hinder your spirit from receiving all that God wants to offer you. He chose you above all else, fully aware of your weaknesses. He died because He wanted you, and not even your sins can separate you from His love.

The confession here is that even though I am a sinner, I am not defined by my sin. I am not a sinner struggling to love God; rather, I am primarily a lover of God who struggles with sin. Both David and Peter were men who truly loved God, yet they both sinned in drastic ways. But instead of letting their weakness control their lives, they trusted in the love of Christ and pushed forward in His plans for them. Choose to believe that the King desires you even in your weakness. He has set His affections on you, and His gaze will not be moved.

Prayer: Heavenly Bridegroom, I choose to believe that what You say about me is truth. I confess that even though I am weak, in Your eyes I am altogether lovely. Your love saved me from my sins so I could be near You—all because You delighted in me. I choose to believe that my sins do not characterize who I am; rather what You say about me defines who I am. I will run to You in times of struggle instead of away from You, and I will let You make me clean.

Day 7 – Expressions of the Father's Heart and Affections

Song of Songs 1:12

While the king is at his table...

Jesus the King expresses the revelation of the affectionate Father's heart to the Bride. He provides a table. He embraces and affirms her at His table. He feeds her spirit on the revelation of who He is and what He did. His table is the revelation of the cross, the reality that she partakes of the free gift of redemption. There is an abundance of food at His table, and that is why when we forget the King's table, our spirit starves. Shame and guilt begin to weigh us down, and we feel as though we can no longer seek His face or draw near to His presence.

"Present yourselves to God as being alive from the dead (Romans 6:13)." In other words, worship God as one who is fully accepted and embraced by the affection of God. Do not allow yourself to be weighed down with condemnation or with fear of rejection. Come to His table and partake of all that He has to give you. Come before Him to sit and rest. Drink deeply of His presence and allow your spirit to be fed on His truths. Let the realization of Song of Songs 1:5 (Dark am I, yet lovely) empower your heart to just sit at the table of the King and know that it is where you belong.

Prayer: Great King, I thank You that in all Your kindness You invited me to come near You. You made a table of pleasures and delights just for me. Continue to feed me with words of truth and speak affectionately to my heart. I choose to trust Your authority over my life because You have been good to me.

Day 8 – A Response to the Father's Affections and the King's Provision

Song of Songs 1:12-14

My spikenard sends forth its fragrance, a bundle of myrrh is my Beloved to me, that lies all night between my breasts. My Beloved is to me a cluster of henna blooms in the vineyards of En Gedi.

The Lord enjoys the fragrance that emanates from your spirit when you are focused on His provision in your life. What He feeds you at His table produces a perfume that ascends from your spirit to God. When the revelation of His table touches you, your perfume ascends spontaneously and effortlessly to the Lord.

Worship is a fragrance that ascends to God as perfume. The Lord enjoys the aroma and fragrance that emanates from your spirit when you are seated at the Lord's Table. *"My spikenard sends forth its fragrance..."* Spikenard speaks of spontaneous worship.

Your fragrance will be diffused to God and man when you begin to receive freely all that Jesus provides. The church at Corinth was one of the most carnal churches in the New Testament, but Paul declared to them, "We *are* the fragrance of Jesus Christ to God the Father (2 Cor. 2:15)."

In other words, when God smells the fragrance of your life, He smells the literal fragrance of His Son. Jesus Christ has a literal fragrance that is a part of His divine Person, and that fragrance is so sweet to the Father.

"...God who... through us diffuses the fragrance of His knowledge in every place. For we are to God the fragrance of Christ among those who are being saved and among those who are perishing. To the one we are the aroma of death leading to death, and to the other the aroma of life leading to life (2 Cor. 2:14-16)..."

Prayer: *Sweet Father, as the fragrance of my lifestyle of worship begins to arise to You, reveal Your delighted heart to me. I was created to worship You in all that I do, so even in my weakness come and enjoy all that I have to give. Thank You for allowing me to impart the precious fragrance of Your Son.*

Day 9 – Oh, How Beautiful You Are!

Song of Songs 1:15

How beautiful you are, my darling. Oh, How Beautiful!

As long as you feel dirty or ashamed, you will draw back from the presence of God. Jesus now adds to the threefold experience of worship, meditation and fragrance (1:12-14). This is necessary groundwork before you can accept a far more difficult truth—you are completely beautiful to God. This is an amazing truth, but it is not easily grasped by the human heart. It is a difficult truth to establish in the private prayer life, but it is a very crucial one. We must not be content until God's people can say in private prayer with a spirit of liberty, "I am so beautiful to Jesus; I am His true love."

The revelation of the beauty of the corporate Church heals relationships. We sometimes feel the Church is ugly and dirty, but remember that God looks at the very same people and proclaims, "Oh, how Beautiful!" Even the Believers that bring grief to us are beautiful to God in Jesus. In seasons of relational difficulty, one of the most preserving truths in our heart is that God is ravished for all Christians, even the ones who mistreat us.

Some of us must reassess how we view the Bride of Christ because she is dark of heart but still lovely to God. The more you see and understand God's heart of love towards you, the easier it will be to see God's ravished heart for others. When you understand that His heart is overwhelmed by you, you can believe that His heart is overwhelmed by others. This gives us much greater patience for our brothers and sisters. God is a God that sees weak people as beautiful to Him in the grace of Jesus.

He says, "You are *beautiful*."

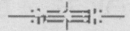

Prayer: *Sweet Father, I thank You that even in my weakness You consider me lovely. Even in the darkness of my heart, You have chosen to love me and You have set Your affections on me. Let this amazing truth open up my soul that I might love You and others the way You love me.*

Day 10 – Gazing on God With Dove's Eyes

Song of Songs 1:15

...You have dove's eyes.

Starting with Noah, the dove has been a picture of the Holy Spirit throughout Scripture. A dove speaks of singleness of purpose because it does not have peripheral vision. Because a dove can only see straight ahead, its focus is clearly set on the object in front of it; a dove's eyes cannot focus on two things at the same time (Matt 6:22).

Also, doves reveal singleness of devotion because they only have one mate throughout their lifetime. Doves are totally faithful in mating. If one dies, the other will never mate again.

"Dove's eyes" speak of the ability to see redemptive truths. Jesus views you as one with singleness of vision; single-mindedness in grace instead of feeling secure one moment, then condemned the next.

The Lord is saying, "I love you, for your eyes see the truth. They look only to Me and not to anything or anyone else. Even in your weakness, your heart is focused on Me. Your eyes are faithful because you trust in My truths. Your gaze is steady on Me!"

These are affirming words intended to give strength to your heart so that you will continue to go hard after God. He wants you to succeed and be faithful to Him, so He gives encouraging words to His Beloved. He wants you to seek Him with all of your heart, mind and soul so He proclaims goodness over your life.

Prayer: *Divine Lover, give me dove's eyes for only You. Let the things of this world become out of focus in comparison to the greatness of Your beauty in my eyes. Change my heart and set my gaze on You. I long to be a wholehearted, single-minded lover of God.*

Day 11 – Response to God's Desires Over Her Beauty

Song of Songs 1:16

Behold, you are handsome, my Beloved! Yes, pleasant! Also our bed is green.

This is the three-fold response to the fact that God has just said, "You are beautiful, you are beautiful, you have dove's eyes." This is a bride overcome with how wonderful it is to be loved as expressed in verse 15.

In response to this, the Bride has a revelation of Jesus' beauty and the spiritual pleasures found in Jesus. "Behold, You are handsome, my Beloved! Yes, pleasant."

His loveliness penetrates the spirit. He is becoming more and more beautiful in the eyes of His Bride as she sees Him more clearly. When the Lord says, "You are beautiful—I love you," it awakens a new depth of revelation of how winsome He is.

Let this be pleasant to the very depths of your heart. Allow your heart to be fascinated with Him as you behold His beauty. There is an exchange of deep affection going back and forth between your heart and His throughout 1:12-17. It is a fellowship in the Holy Spirit with a spontaneous flow of His heart to yours and your heart back to Him.

When Jesus appears handsome and pleasant to the soul of a Believer, full obedience seems so reasonable. When we connect with the fact that He enjoys us, we start to enjoy Him. When we have revelation of His beauty, we begin to see how beautiful we are to Him. With such revelation upon our hearts, we more easily give up things that once were distractions for us. No longer do we count them as great sacrifices to forego, but rather we feel joy as we yield ourselves more fully to Him.

"Behold, You are handsome... Also, our bed is green." The bed speaks of rest and security without fear of judgment or rejection from Jesus. The declaration is, "I'm resting in security on the green bed of the Lord." The New American Standard translates it as, "Our luxuriant couch." The couch of the Lord is plush, green and filled with life. Whether on the Lord's bed or couch, she is nonetheless seated with Him in heavenly places (Eph. 2:16).

Resting in God flourishes, prospers and brings vibrancy, instead of leaving you parched and barren like a desert. Rest in the love of God because the abundance of His love is great!

Prayer: *Beautiful Man, overwhelm my heart with the depth of Your awesome beauty. Cause the depth of Your graces to penetrate my being and resound throughout my spirit. I long to see You as You really are, so show me Your glory! Let me rest safely in the abundance of Your love for me.*

Day 12 – Revelation of the Father's Beautiful Inheritance for His Son, Part 1

Song of Songs 2:1

I am the rose of Sharon and the lily of the valley.

The first great confession is, "I'm dark, but lovely (1:5)." We see Jesus' beauty and then we see how Jesus gave His beauty to us. Then He gives us His couch and His house, and now we are prepared to grasp another dimension of our identity.

The second great confession is, "I am the rose of Sharon; I am the lily of the valley." In this revelation, you see yourself as resting on a flourishing couch in a beautiful house that is eternally permanent and made in strength. You are discovering a deeper dimension of who you are in Jesus.

I believe this is the highest identity as the Bride of Christ. This revelation can only be discerned by first having a good foundation in understanding the redemptive riches in Christ (1:12-17).

This confession is more than the fact that you are lovely and desired by God, for it goes even higher. You are now the inheritance that the Father has promised His only Son. It is one thing to enjoy someone deeply, but it is another thing when this person is your eternal inheritance. This is the confession that comes from the understanding that you are *the* only inheritance that the Father has promised His Son— you are the prize, a bride pictured as a rose.

"I am the inheritance God has promised His Son. There is only one rose, one beauty, that Jesus Christ longs for and that rose is me!" Understand that you are the rose that intoxicates and captures the heart of Christ Jesus, and know that you are more than loved by God. Declaring these truths about yourself allows your heart to comprehend them more completely and brings you deeper in your walk with God. His Word says that this is who you are, and when you come into agreement with what He says about you, your heart begins to unlock.

***

Prayer: *Jesus, I thank You that You have spoken this truth over my life, and I choose to accept Your words. Even though I am dark, You say I am lovely in Your eyes. I am a rose in the midst of thorns, and my weakness does not define who I am. You say I am lovely, so I will choose to believe that in Your eyes I am beautiful.*

Day 13 – Revelation of the Father's Beautiful Inheritance for His Son, Part 2

Song of Songs 2:1

I am the rose of Sharon and the lily of the valleys.

This is an essential revelation even at the beginning of the journey—her new identity as the only pure Bride in Jesus. The picture of the lily represents purity. She makes this next confession, "I am the only thing in the world that is pure in God's sight." There is only one lily in God's purpose. While the New International Version says, "I am *a* rose and *a* lily," I prefer *the* rose and *the* lily, as most of the other versions have done.

She is the lily of the valley. The valleys speak of the low and dark places in this fallen world. She says, "When God looks, He only sees one thing pure in all the Earth: The Bride of Christ!" She says, "In the sight of God, I understand I am *the* lily amidst the fallen valley of this dark world."

She is not confused by thinking all the darkness of her heart is gone. But the negative is not predominant in her eyes. The Church (Bride) of Christ is the only thing that God esteems as innocent and pure in His sight in this fallen world. She feels clean, innocent and pure before Jesus.

Prayer: Lord, thank You that this is who I am, that my identity is found in Your eyes, and You see me as Your pure and spotless Bride. Even in the midst of this fallen world, You look upon me with eyes of love and have called me Your own. I have been made pure with Your love.

Day 14 – Nourishment and Provision that Leads to Rest and Joy in His Presence

Song of Songs 2:4b

He brought me to the banqueting house, and His banner over me was love.

This verse speaks of the divine nourishment and provision that leads us to rest in joy. Other versions use the word "banqueting table." The wine house is where the celebration is, where the Lord brings us to rejoice in the celebration of His love."

There is a table at the end of our journey, which is the full banqueting table. The Bride touched the banqueting house in 2:1 when she said, "I am the rose, I am His queen, I am His Bride, and I am His inheritance." It is this revelation that is bringing her to the banqueting table. It is the knowledge of how He feels towards her, that she is His exceedingly great reward at the end of the age.

This confession—"His banner over me is love"—brings healing and refreshment to her. This is the delightful banner that she sees over her life. This is her confession when she fails, and this is her confession when she is in a time of temptation, not just the shame of failure, but also in the presence of temptations. This is her confession when she's under great pressure. The banner of God is going to bring you love in all the difficult circumstances. His banner over you is love, not neglect. How amazing!

The banner of His love defines her life when she succeeds and when she fails. His banner is always love. God's love means that she can have the confidence in His loving mercy in her weakness. The banner over her life is not rejection when she fails; it is always love. And she can stand before the Lord and say, "You love me. I am beloved of God, even when I fail." She might have been ensnared in immorality (1:6, the veiled woman), but she confesses God's love over her failures. When we stumble, the Lord's dealing in our life is always love.

Prayer: Lord, You have called me to Your banqueting table and have given me the privilege of partaking of the inheritance with the saints. Thank You for feeding my heart and giving me the privilege of joining with You in Your inheritance. You have brought me near, and in this place, I am satisfied.

Day 15 – Lovesick

Song of Songs 2:5

Sustain me with cakes of raisins; refresh me with apples, for I am lovesick.

Now comes the longing to enjoy more experiences of the depths of Jesus. "Sustain me with cakes of raisins. Refresh me with apples." In other words, crying out, "Give me more of God!" The cakes of raisins speak of the Holy Spirit. Raisins are forms of grapes, which are used to make wine. This speaks of the ministry of the Holy Spirit even though it is a lesser form of the flowing wine. With more fervency than ever before, the Bride is saying, "Even if it is just a taste, I have to have more of the Holy Spirit. I don't care what the amount, just give me more of my Lover." The revelation of God's affection for her has produced an earnest seeking.

The Lord is drawing her. Feelings of love can sometimes be so intense that a larger amount of sustenance is needed. "Sustain me," reveals her confidence to ask for more, "...for I am lovesick." He is making her lovesick to prepare her to press on to maturity. He is making her lovesick so she never desires to go back again.

One aspect of seeking God involves the release of the presence of God upon our hearts. When our hearts are tenderized, we feel love from God and we are then able to open up and let our love flow back to God. We were made in such a way that we love to feel we're giving ourselves wholeheartedly to God.

This is a wonderful manifestation of the presence of God in us. This cry is an intense desire for just one more touch, just one more glimpse, just one more taste. I am longing for more of the beauty of God. How amazing is this desire! It is absolutely necessary to sustain true intimacy.

Prayer: *Oh awesome Lover, come and sustain my heart in all situations, for I am lovesick for You. Only Your perfect love will satisfy my heart's desire. Refresh me with more and more of Your love, and draw me closer to where You are. My heart's desire is to know Your love!*

Day 16 – Experiencing God's Embrace

Song of Songs 2:6

His left hand is under my head, and his right hand embraces me.

This is a picture of God continuing to draw her closer. She has so much confidence in the love of God in this season that she allows herself to rest in His arms.

The left hand represents the invisible activity of God. The left hand of God is behind her head, so it is felt but not seen. It speaks of the activity of God in your life that you are not aware of. The invisible activity of God in your life is a very important expression of God's love for you. God is both withholding and releasing events that you cannot discern, however they are present just the same. The Lord is sparing you from troubles and pains that you are not aware of because it is away from your view.

The left-hand activity of God is something you accept by faith. It really is an important part of our worship before the Lord. Not that we must daily recognize or see each detail of His activity in our lives; that is not the point. There are just so many things withheld from us that would have caused anguish, fear, worry and pain. Yet in His mercy and grace, He allowed them to be hidden from your knowing. Oh, how good is His love towards us!

Prayer: *God, cause me to recognize Your just dealings in my life. Thank You for always being there for me and for embracing me in all times. Let me daily believe that You are working in my life for the better, even though I do not see Your hand.*

Day 17 – Revelation of Jesus as the Fearless Lover

Song of Songs 2:8

The voice of my Beloved! Behold, He comes leaping upon the mountains, skipping upon the hills.

Here the young Bride has an entirely new revelation of Jesus as the sovereign King. She sees Jesus as the Lord of all who effortlessly conquers all opposing mountains. Up until this time, she only understood Jesus as the counseling shepherd and the affectionate Father who lovingly fed her grapes and apples from His table. Now she is beholding yet another aspect of His beauty as He is skipping and leaping on mountains.

Jesus is seen as the Lord of the nations and all things; Jesus, the King, overcomes opposition—effortlessly. *Mountains* speak of human or demonic obstacles that hinder her full faith and obedience towards Him.

In Mark 11:23, Jesus taught us to speak to the "mountains of adversity," commanding them to move. "...Whoever says to this mountain, 'Be removed and be cast into the sea,' and does not doubt in his heart, but believes that those things he says will be done, he will have whatever he says." Many times the Scripture speaks of mountains in context to natural and spiritual governments. Since a mountain is very large and immovable, it provides a good picture of government. Why? Because a government is very large and unmovable; for all intents and purposes, it is permanent. Nevertheless, He declares with His actions that the obstacles in the world are as nothing before Him—human, demonic, governmental, natural, spiritual, seen or unseen. He is *always* victorious over obstacles.

Prayer: *Conquering King, I thank You for Your wisdom and strength over the mountains that arise in life. I thank You that You are the chief conqueror and that through You all things are possible. Teach me to abide in Your strength, and lean into Your mercy more and more every day.*

Day 18 – Jesus as the Strong Gazelle

Song of Songs 2:8c-9a

He comes leaping upon the mountains, skipping upon the hills. My beloved is like a gazelle or a young stag.

This is yet another new revelation of Jesus; this is another light of His countenance that she has not yet beheld. She sees Him as a gazelle or a young stag leaping and skipping on mountains. Jesus is pictured in His effortless victory over all His enemies and all their authority, whether on the Earth or in the heavens (Col. 1:13). He is seated far above all power, thrones, dominions and names (Eph. 1:22). He has authority over all nations. Jesus is revealed as leaping over these enemies with ease in His victorious, resurrected life.

A gazelle is an animal that is especially swift in its sudden energetic movements. Since a gazelle can run easily in the high places, it is the picture of effortless ascension up the mountain. The heavenly Stag speaks of fearlessly conquering all opposition, not the fragile and easily distracted gazelle that is described in verse seven.

This is a new revelation of Jesus as a triumphant leaping gazelle with unlimited energy and agility to overcome obstacles. This gazelle is fast and swift, with tremendous movement as it leaps from place to place. Because this is another new revelation of Jesus, this is also another new way in which she is required to trust and obey Him. Before it was the counseling Shepherd and the comforting King, but now it is the fearless lover who is leaping and bounding over seemingly impossible obstacles. Her loyalties now are to be towards a triumphant leader who shows no fear and holds nothing back. Again, the Bride must request grace to submit and obey.

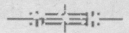

Prayer: Mighty Lord, to Your power and might, all the obstacles in my life must bow. Lord, come take my hand and teach me to leap with You like a gazelle over the mountains in my life. Guide me through all the obstructions that I face, and direct my feet so that I can be like You, conquering all opposition.

Day 19 – God's Gaze Through the Lattice

Song of Songs 2:9c-d

He is looking through the window, gazing through the lattice.

When God created each individual person, He built a wall with strategic openings so that only He could deeply touch that person in a specific way. No one else knows where these special windows are, and no one else knows how to touch each individual human heart the way that God does.

The *windows* and *lattice* speak of openings in the strategic wall that God builds around each of us. In other words, the wall is His strategic, personalized plan to train us in bridal partnership. His divine plan focuses on the best way to reach and awaken your heart in the deepest way possible. The wall speaks of the ways where you, in a holy way, are vulnerable to Jesus touching your life; the Lord has purposed to transform your heart in ways that only He can. He is wooing you and calling you into a deeper love. He is gazing at His Bride—at you—right now.

Jesus continues the Divine romance as He trains your heart in intimacy. He will not stop pursuing you, and He will not stop gazing. For His eyes are set on a prize, and that prize is you—His eternal Bride promised to Him from the beginning of creation! His focus will not be distracted, for He is truly, madly, deeply in love with you, and He will win the affections of your heart even though it takes death.

Open up your soul to the deep longings of Christ towards you. Be refreshed in your spirit and energized in your inner man, knowing that the fearless Lover adores you!

Prayer: *God, thank You for the openings and the windows You have created in my life. Transform my heart through the purity of Your loving gaze towards me. Draw me into bridal partnership with You as You continue to woo me with Your love.*

Day 20 – Actions Drawing Her Into Mature Partnership

Song of Songs 2:10

My lover spoke to me, "Arise, my darling, my beautiful one, and come with me."

He is calling her to come away with Him, to leap and skip over the mountains. Jesus wants His Bride to agree and join with Him in all of His doings. He is asking her to step out of her comfort zone and leave her place of familiarity to partner with Him.

What He is calling her to do is frightening and uncertain to her. It is a step that will force her to trust and obey Him completely. She feels as if she doesn't like the risks of walking by faith. She does not want to go to the high places because she is afraid of the mountains.

Faith is the way of the Kingdom. God, in His infinite wisdom, has ordained a Kingdom that operates by absolute confidence in the invisible things of God (2 Cor. 5:7; 4:18). The way of faith is a mysterious way to operate a Kingdom; however, God, who is perfect in knowledge, desires a Bride for His Son who is willing to take His hand with confidence and partner with Him in all His decisions. The foundation of the Kingdom *must* be founded on confidence in God. We honor our Lord when we have confidence in His integrity, even though we can't feel or see anything. It reflects devotion and commitment, much more than seeing and feeling does.

The young Bride did not yet want to be a warrior. She wanted to sit under the shade tree for the rest of her life and enjoy loving and worshipping Jesus. She did not want to war against darkness, yet God wants a worshipping, warring

Bride. He wants us to both love and fight, because He is a warrior and He is a lover (Ps. 62:11-12).

Prayer: Father, help me to become a warrior as well as a worshipper. Even through my own inner fears and weaknesses, teach me to walk in faith and to not be afraid of risking it all for the sake of knowing You. Teach me how to choose Your ways in faith, even if I have to leave other things behind to follow You. My desire is to be a Bride who will partner with Your Son in all His journeys and decisions.

Day 21 – Encouraged by Signs of Fruitfulness

Song of Songs 2:11-13

For lo, the winter is past, the rain is over and gone. The flowers appear on the earth; the time of singing has come, and the voice of the turtledove is heard in our land. The fig tree puts forth her green figs, and the vines with the tender grapes give a good smell. Rise up, my love, my fair one, and come away!

Jesus prophetically encourages her by telling her that it is the time for fruitfulness. The Lord is equipping her to overcome fear so that she will be able to follow Him. She is still immature in her understanding that He is a trustworthy God. The prophetic signs are right before her. It is springtime in the Spirit. He is warning her that the season of harvest is not far away, so she must learn to trust and obey Him right now.

He encourages her by recalling how He has been faithful to her in past winter seasons. He reminds her that He helped her in the cold bitter winter before, and He promises to be with her the in following seasons. Winter is symbolic of trials, just as the north winds are (4:16a). Very few things grow in the harsh winter. The winter season is dark, cold and difficult. However, the fruitfulness from the winter season is now apparent in her life, as shown by the fig, a winter fruit (2:13a).

He is saying, "I helped you in your past trials (the dark of winter). Why do you think I'll forget you when we go up the mountain together? Why are you so afraid? Why are you hiding behind that wall? The winter is past, and I am the One who took you through it."

He is saying, "If we were together throughout past difficulties, we will be together in the future ones. I want you to be with Me; I want you to trust Me."

One reason the Lord takes us through difficult seasons is to give us our own personal history in the faithfulness of God. In these times He gives us reasons to trust His decisions, and He teaches us how to be confident in His love.

Prayer: *God, You have been so faithful to me! In Your grace, continue to encourage and equip my heart through a deeper revelation of the times and seasons of my life. You have taken me through the hard times, so now take me into a time of singing. I will say yes when You call me to come away with You, and yes to our future together in Your enduring goodness.*

Day 22 – Embraced in Her Weakness

Song of Songs 2:14

Oh my dove, in the clefts of the rock, in the secret places of the cliff, let me see your face, let me hear your voice, for your voice is sweet, and your face is lovely.

The Lord reveals His tender heart of affection as He declares her beauty even while she struggles with fear. He calls her to have confidence in a time of weakness. He already knows in verse 14 that He will be refused in verse 17. Like Peter, the Lord could say to her, "I know that you will deny Me three times due to your fear. I know that your flesh is weak, but I also know that you have a willing spirit (Matt. 26:41). The words, "Oh, My dove," reveal the tenderness of God's heart. He knows that in a matter of moments she will give in to compromise, yet still He calls her His dove. He proclaims, "I know you are struggling, but you are still *My* dove."

A dove is a guileless bird representing purity, innocence and loyalty since it never mates after its partner dies. Thus, they are unique in loyalty. He didn't call her a deceitful snake, but rather His dove. He is endeared by her sincerity. He knows that her heart and flesh are weak, but she is sincere in her affections towards Him. God sees her through the finished work of the cross and embraces her in her fear with tender affection.

Prayer: Lord, in my weakness, continue to declare the tenderness of Your heart toward me. My heart is overjoyed by the reality of Your desire toward me even during my struggle. Embrace me in my fears and see through all of my immaturity so that the truth about who You say I am would become fully alive in my heart.

Day 23 – The Safety of Christ Crucified

Song of Songs 2:14a

Oh My dove, in the clefts of the rock...

Jesus is the rock of God. A rock is unchanging; it is a strong and durable foundational material. In First Corinthians 10:14, Paul taught that Jesus was the spiritual Rock that followed the nation of Israel in Moses' day. "...they drank of that spiritual Rock that followed them, and that Rock was Christ..."

The "cleft of the rock" is the place where God hid Moses when he caused His glory to pass by. The glory of God kills sinful human flesh. Because it is so pure, Moses would have died if he saw God face-to-face. Therefore, the Lord created a cleft, or an open space in the mountain. The Lord hid Moses in this cleft, and then put His hand over him to protect him as He passed by. This was a foreshadowing of redemption.

The Rock that protects us from God's glory breaking out against our sinfulness is Jesus Christ. The suffering and death of Christ is the cleft of the Rock where we are hidden. This is the only safe place the Father has provided from which we are to relate to Him; His desire is that we would hide in the cleft of salvation, calling for His nearness.

Prayer: Jesus, thank You for the wounds in your side and the holes in Your hands, for they provide me with shelter during times of trial. Only You are my rock, and I will hide myself in the shadow of Your wings.

Day 24 – Prayer for Deliverance From Compromise

Song of Songs 2:15

Catch us the foxes, the little foxes that spoil the vines...

The Bride's plea for help with the little foxes is a prayer for deliverance. You can feel the sincerity of her heart as she cries out desperately. Though immature, she realizes her weaknesses and beseeches the Lord.

Foxes are cunning little animals that destroy the vineyards in Israel under the cover of night; they are not bold lions that attack during the day. They are subtle, crafty, and prove difficult to catch. Carnal believers often miss catching the "little foxes" in their lives. They catch the lions, but not the foxes. The Lord wants to partner with us to capture the compromises that are out to destroy our hearts.

She longs for help, and asks the Lord to catch the little areas of compromise and fear in her life, which she does not yet know how to subdue. She says, "I don't live in immorality anymore. I'm not a disgraced woman. However, my problems are now more subtle." The foxes in her life are no longer sins of *commission*; they are sins of *omission*.

She cries, "Lord, we are in this together. Catch these crafty destroyers of my relationship with You! They escape too quickly. I can't catch them by myself." We must also pray continually for the Lord's help in these areas, for He desires to help us. As Jesus said, "Let me see your face; let Me hear your voice."

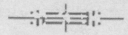

Prayer: *God, I confess that I have little foxes at work in my life. Release your Holy Spirit to come and catch all the compromises of my heart. As you apprehend these compromises, release greater fruitfulness in me. Remove everything in my life that hinders love.*

Day 25 – Painful Compromise

Song of Songs 2:16-17

My lover is mine and I am his; he browses among the lilies. Until the day breaks and the shadows flee, turn, my lover, and be like a gazelle or like a young stag on the rugged hills.

Now sincere love is expressed. The Bride declares that she belongs only to Jesus. She is proclaiming with confidence that she has not lost her place in the heart of God. She knows that Jesus is still hers, and that she belongs to Him. She is not just loved and cherished by Christ, but she belongs solely to Him and no other.

This is the reality that she is truly starting to accept. She is allowing herself to take her place as the Bride of Christ and profess that she is His. She is a lover of God, and God loves her even in her weaknesses. She is committed and sincere even if she is not yet fully victorious or mature.

However, despite her beginning to understand this truth, she still chooses not to follow Him over the mountains. She bids Him to go on without her. She is refusing to obey Him, not because she is rebellious or because she is a hopeless hypocrite, but because she is spiritually immature.

It is dark until the day breaks and brings new light. The time when day breaks is the time when light or maturity becomes present. She is telling Him that she wants His help to conquer theses areas in her heart so she can go on to the mountains with Him. She doesn't want to go to the mountains until the light of day comes and shadows, or the gray areas, are gone.

She is telling Him that she still has unbelief in her heart, but she wants His light to come and take it away. She says, "God, unless there is more light and I am more mature, You are going to have to turn and go on without me. I cannot rise until the shadows have fled."

This happens to many Christians during their spiritual journey. They decline when Christ asks them to partner with Him, and because of this, they feel as if they are hopeless hypocrites. They doubt their sincerity towards Christ, and they wonder if they even love Him the way that they thought they did. Then they begin to run away from the things of God instead of toward the things of God.

This is what Satan wants the beloved to do. He wants her mistakes to conquer her instead of causing her to run to God for help. Mistakes do not disqualify you from being with Christ; they qualify you to run *to* Christ. This does not mean you should try to sin and make mistakes, but it does mean that even if you slip and fall in a time of weakness, you should get right back up and run back to the love of Christ.

Ask Christ to shine the light of His countenance down upon your life so the shadows of fear and doubt would flee and the gray areas of immaturity would become as light. Ask Him to give you grace that allows you to run to Him in times of struggle.

Prayer: Sweet Jesus, I thank You that I belong wholly to You. Even in my times of difficulty, You accept me as I am. Come and shine the light of Your beauty down upon my life that all my sins would flee away. Give me the grace I need to follow You in times of struggle, for You are mine and I am Yours.

Day 26 – The Bridegroom's Manifest Presence is Withdrawn

Song of Solomon 3:1

By night on my bed I sought the one I love; I sought Him, but I did not find Him.

She told Him to go to the mountain without her, and now His manifest presence in her life is gone. He is still with her, but she cannot feel His immediate presence with her the way she did before.

It is a new experience for her to seek after Him and not find Him. This was her own doing, however, because she chose not to obey His biddings to join with Him. She stayed behind her wall of isolation praying on her bed (her place of rest and comfort). She preferred to sit under the shade tree and eat grapes and raisin cakes instead of following Him.

Because He loves her too much to leave her in a position of disobedience, Jesus refuses to come to her until she obeys Him. He is now absent from her presence, and she is alone. She was sincere in her love and affections for Him, but she is not ready to give up her place of comfort to enter into new levels of partnership.

This love will eventually drive her to pursue Him passionately, but unless she is left without His presence, she will have no reason to leave the security of her bed. She may feel alone and forgotten, but He continues to woo her to come away with Him. Just because His presence is not manifest doesn't mean He is not beckoning her to arise. Rather, the lack of His Spirit near her will eventually drive her to pursue the One she loves.

This is the Bridegroom's pure divine strategy to stir up His Bride. He wants her to discover for herself that the only safe and perfect place is in partnership with Him. Wherever He goes, no matter where He goes, this is where His Bride should be. We should be completely dependant on Him, and if we are not willing to be dependent on Him, then He will hide Himself for a time until we are ready to agree with His decisions.

Seek the Lord, but don't just seek Him like you did in other seasons of your life. Seek Him in the night seasons as well as the day, when you feel His presence and when you do not. Isaiah 64:7 says, "Is there anyone who calls upon God's name, who stirs Himself up to take hold of God?" There is a time to stir yourself up to take hold of God because sometimes God *does* hide His face until we seek Him. However, He promises that if you seek Him with all of your heart, you will find Him. He will be found by you.

Prayer: *Father, train me to stir up my spirit to take hold of Your Son. There are times when I feel Him near me and times when I do not, but I want the fullness of God living inside of me. I want to be able to partner with Your Son in all He does. I praise You, Lord, because I know that if I seek You with all of my heart, You will reveal Yourself to me.*

Day 27 – Driven by Love to Seek the One She Loves

Song of Songs 3:2, 4

"I will rise now," I said, "and go about the city; in the streets and in the squares, I will seek the One I love..." Scarcely had I passed by them, when I found the One I love. I held Him and would not let Him go...

Now she is driven by love and arises to seek for Him. She has been without His presence for too long, and she must get up to go out and find Him. She is exactly where He wanted her to be; she is now willing to leave her comfort zone and search for her Beloved—something she was unwilling to do before He removed His Spirit from her. The disappointment of losing His presence motivates her to rise and leave the security of her bed. "You will seek me and find me when you seek me with all your heart. I will be found by you, declares the Lord (Jeremiah 29:13-14)."

Our fears are conquered as we take the first steps in obeying God's commands. It is our inheritance to be free from any and all fear that binds us. The Lord is zealous for our full agreement in partnership, and He desires us to overcome every fear that restrains us.

The Bride realized that prayer alone would not solve the situation; it required her active obedience. She is now willing to obey Him actively, as she stirs her inner man to arise and look for Him in the streets. Because she is now actively trying to find Him, He renews His presence. It is a response to her obedience and a token of His promises to her.

The key thing here is that she stirred herself to leave her comfort zone and find her Beloved. She sought after Him not only with prayer but also with obedience to His calling upon her life. When she did feel His presence again, she vowed never to let Him go again. She committed her spirit to obey Him always—no matter what it took. She longed to have the majestic God as her one and only love.

This is where God wants our hearts to be—in a place of contending for His presence in our life. Will we fight on behalf of the one that we love? Will we wrestle with God like Jacob did? We do not have to live bored in God. He longs to fascinate and captivate every part of our being. He is asking you to obey and seek Him out, and in return, He promises that you *will* find Him!

Prayer: *Holy God, this day I choose to arise and leave it all behind to find You. I long for You in the night and in the day. Send Your spirit to strengthen my inner man to contend for Your presence. I long to know You and to be fascinated by Your beauty. I will arise today and search for the One I love. I will seek You with all of my heart, mind, soul and strength.*

Day 28 – Revelation of Jesus as a Safe Savior

Song of Songs 3:6

Who is this coming out of the wilderness like pillars of smoke, perfumed with myrrh and frankincense, with all the merchant's fragrant powders?

The wilderness is symbolic of life in this fallen age. Israel's 40-year journey through the wilderness is a picture of our struggle in a fallen world while on our way to the Promised Land filled with the glory of God. The wilderness is a time of difficulty and intense testing. The wilderness is a place that represents a time of failure and sin—a season where sin and the flesh wage war against our spirit. It is a season of spiritual warfare against the enemy.

However, it also is a place of encounter with God. Jesus spent 33 years on Earth in the wilderness of this fallen world. He laid aside the form of God, and He took upon Himself the form of creation. He left the eternal city to descend into a depressed, sinful world filled with demons and oppression. This world was a wilderness for Him. Jesus was a man who was highly acquainted with the wilderness. He was in the desert for forty days, endured testing in the garden of Gethsemane, and, most powerful of all, suffered death on a cross. However, unless there were not these times of testing and hardship in the desert, victory would not have seemed so sweet.

"Who is this *coming out of* the wilderness like pillars of smoke...?" Who is this coming up victorious over the fallen world? In this picture, it is describing Jesus as being triumphant over the wilderness, but in the end (Song of Songs 8:5), it is the Bride who is now triumphant over the wilderness. We need to know that Jesus experienced and conquered the fallen world so that our own hearts may be empowered to do the same. He knows our pain because He Himself had to endure the wilderness. When we realize that God can relate to us on this level, it strengthens us to rise up and fight to conquer sins and darkness in our own lives.

He doesn't just stand at a distance, commanding us to come to Him. He experienced human life in this fallen world, and He knows what we are going through in our quest to come up out of the wilderness victoriously.

Jesus not only conquered this world, He did it in glory. Smoke speaks of the glory and wonder of God. It is a manifestation of God's holy presence, and it is associated with the fire of the Holy Spirit. Jesus is now victorious and clothed in the smoke of the glory of God. He ascended out of the wilderness wrapped in heavenly garments, displaying the wonder of God's glory.

This is where we are headed—this is our inheritance! We were called to be victorious with Christ, wrapped in heavenly garments with Him. He died so we could partner with Him in His victory over the things of this world. Jesus did it all to secure our safety, our eternal life with Him as His Bride. He will bring us up out of the wilderness, victorious in love!

Prayer: *Jesus, I thank You that in Your mercy, You came down to Earth and became a man. You obeyed Your Father and left everything behind, rising above the obstacles and the wilderness of this fallen world. I thank You that You were victorious over death and victorious in this fallen age. Because You conquered this world, I too can conquer the things of this Earth. Grant me grace to be like You, so that I might come up out of the desert triumphant over my sins.*

Day 29 – You are His Crown of Glory

Song of Solomon 3:11

Go forth, Oh daughters of Zion, and see the King Solomon with the crown with which His mother crowned Him on the day of His wedding, the day of the gladness of His heart.

"See Him crowned as King on His wedding day," is an exhortation for her to see herself as the inheritance of the Lord. It is an encouragement for her to see who she is as the Bride of Christ. The final triumph is described as the wedding day between Jesus and the Church. She also is pleading with the daughters who are the more immature ones. "See what I have seen. He has been crowned King with full authority. He will only have the gladness of His heart if His people are His Bride on that day."

There is a crown that He longs for more than any other crown. He wants the crown of the voluntary love of His Bride. He has many crowns, but this is the crown we crown Him with. He will be crowned "on His wedding day." That is the crown He is waiting for. There will be a day when the Church from throughout all history will crown Him as King with their love.

The Church crowns Jesus as King when they respond to His kingship in a personal way. This is the day when, in all fullness, we become the Bride. This is the day that is the true gladness of His heart. He is receiving the gladness of the Bridegroom. This is the great purpose of it all. There is a Man whose name is Jesus, and He will have a Bride at the end of the age.

It is all about a wedding between the Son of God and His eternal Bride, the Church. This day is the gladness of His heart. This is the great reality of all eternity! When we meet our Maker face to face, we will no longer call Him our Master, but we will call Him our Husband. Oh, how sweet destiny is when you are the Bride of Christ, when you know the King of all creation intimately and are His friend. This is the great and grand purpose of it all.

Prayer: *Bridegroom of Love, You are the desire of the nations! I will freely give You all my heart and all of my love. I will crown You as the Bridegroom of my heart, and I will be Your Bride. I long for the day when I will meet You face to face as Your exceeding great reward! I love to love You! Come quickly and let us celebrate together the day of the gladness of Your heart!*

Day 30 – Rooted and Grounded as the Bride

Proverbs 16:22

Understanding is a fountain of life to those who have it.

Our goal is to discern and understand holy patterns more clearly and then apply them to our life in practical ways. Understanding is a fountain of life. The patterns found in the Song of Songs will help us locate and identify the issues that God is specifically dealing with in our lives.

He deals with all of us on the exact same principles. However, there are different applications because we all have different needs and seasons in our journey. God uses the same principles to train each of us. When we discover that the pressures and trials of life we experience are common to all of God's people, then we don't feel quite so isolated. We also will be better equipped to discern the seasons of our lives according to this "spiritual map," and the resulting knowledge aids us in our progression to spiritual maturity.

Reading and meditating on the Song of Songs is like opening a window in your soul: it helps encourage and inspire your heart, it feeds your spirit on the truths of the beauty of Christ, and it gives direction for certain situations in your own spiritual journey. Don't be afraid to dive deeper into these realities and set your heart on the things of Heaven. Allow God to speak directly to your inner man, and let Him be your friend in all that you do.

Prayer: Precious Lord, root me and ground me in the revelation of Your Word so that I may have full knowledge of Your works in my life. Grant me a discerning spirit, that I would know the season You have placed me in so I would fully develop all that You have

for me to walk in. Come and be my Friend, my Lover and my Lord.
Amen.

CHAPTER II

Union with the Indwelling Christ

Chris Berglund

Chris and Susan Berglund recently returned to Pasadena, California, after spending the past 15 years in both Kansas City and Seattle. Twenty years ago, while Chris was attending Fuller Theological Seminary, he and Susan joined Che' Ahn and Lou Engle in planting a local church in Pasadena. Then in 1989, the Lord led the Berglunds to join Mike Bickle by moving to Kansas City where Chris began teaching at Grace Training Center. The Berglunds then moved to Seattle where they pastored the Bethlehem Korean Church for four years.

For the past six years Chris has been teaching and imparting a devotional lifestyle of intimacy with the indwelling Christ at the Forerunner School of Ministry (FSM) founded by Mike Bickle. Throughout the past 15 years, Bob and Nina Lyon, a 90-year-old couple who have been living lives of contemplative prayer for 60 years, have mentored Chris and Susan.

Three years ago, Chris and Susan joined The Call School faculty as Deans of Students, in order to co-labor with their covenant friends, Lou and Therese Engle.

If you would like more information on contemplative prayer or how you can sponsor a contemplative retreat in your area, we welcome you to visit their website at www.christwithin.com. If you would like to contact the Berglunds or if you would like more specific information, feel free to email them at cberglund@christwithin.com.

Day 1

1 Thessalonians 5:17

Pray without ceasing.

A true spirit of prayer is born within a heart of love. This prayer of the heart may be too deep for words. In such union, even our sighs and groans are a fragrance of intercession before the throne of Heaven.

Recently, as my friend watched a televised report seeing images of bomb-torn villages and floods of orphans and widows left in the wake of war and conflict in the Middle East, her heart was pierced. She sighed with pain over the plight of those beautiful children and those who came out of the shadows of war to find themselves widows. At the end of this thirty-minute special she said to the Lord, "I suppose I should now pray for the hurting children and these heartbroken women." As clear as she has ever heard the Lord, He responded with His internal voice and said, "You have been praying for the last 30 minutes; I heard every groan, I interpreted every sigh and answered every tear."

For too long we have compartmentalized our prayers and separated them from our hearts! It is absolutely beautiful how we ourselves can "become prayer" as our hearts are joined in union with the Indwelling Christ. This is how we pray without ceasing; even our sighs, groans and tears become prayer. Let us tend to the fires of love within so that the fires on the altar of our hearts ever release the fragrance of intercession before the throne.

***

Prayer: Father, bring us into union with the Indwelling Christ so that the fire on the altar of my heart never goes out. Lord, we put our weak hearts before Your blazing presence and we thank You for purifying everything that hinders love, of everything that creates the faction between "heart" and "prayer." We thank You,

Lord, that as we are found in You, even our sighs and groans become fragrances ascending to the Father. Grace us, Lord, to become prayer for Your glory and for Your honor, we pray.

Day 2

Genesis 15:11

And when the vultures came down on the carcasses, Abram drove them away.

Though Jesus purchased us with His very blood, He does not force His claim over any of us. Rather, He draws us by His Spirit, seeking to bring each one of us into a voluntary yielding of our lives to Him. In Chapter 15 of Genesis we read that upon this altar lay a heifer, a female goat and a ram. Each animal was divided into halves, laid side by side. Now Abram was waiting for the fire from Heaven to consume his offering. During his waiting the birds of the air came down in order to devour the offering. What a prophetic picture of our lives!

We, too, need to place ourselves on His altar, allowing all our inward parts to be exposed so nothing is hidden or concealed. How often have we laid our hearts upon the altar of sacrifice and said to God, "Take me fully and have Your way with me, I am Yours!" This fresh consecration feels so right and so good. Perhaps before the fire of the Lord fell upon the offering of our heart, the birds of prey swooped down. Some of these birds spoke through our friends, others spoke directly to our thought-life: "Take yourself off the altar; God does not require that of you; relax, enjoy life—your current consecration is plenty, God does not expect more of you..." Have you heard such voices come to you after such times of fresh consecration? These voices become clearer and closer together, and sometimes we start to agree with these "birds of prey," and we remove ourselves from the altar of consecration. We call it "grace;" we shout against legalism and all the while our hearts shrink and our ears become dull of hearing. Where are the Abrams that show their deep sincerity of heart by driving away the birds of prey—not letting these times of testing discourage their hearts? With no sacrifice upon the altar, there is no fire

from Heaven! It is the presence of the sacrifice that draws
the heavenly fire!

Prayer: *Father, we ask for a spirit of wisdom and revelation in the
knowledge of Your Son Jesus. We pray that this revelational
empowerment would equip us to stand fast in the day of testing.
Strengthen us in our inner man, dear Lord, so that we would walk
worthy of Your name. We submit to You, Lord, and in doing so
we resist the birds of prey that would entice us with the spirit of
this age and allure us away from wholehearted abandonment to the
One we love.*

Day 3

Habakkuk 2:20

But the Lord is in His Holy Temple. Let all the Earth be silent before Him.

The Lord seldom answers our prayers with the same decibel level in which we prayed them. Often He is only heard in silence. In quietness and confidence we begin to discern the still, small, internal voice of our Lord. There is a silence that is holy, but not because there is nothing to say; rather, it is a silence of love that is too deep to be expressed with words. When we come before the Lord in silence, we are placing ourselves with all our weakness and failures before His great love. We are simply sitting at His feet to receive His love, and in return, to love Him. During such silence we become attuned to His divine heartbeat and our hearts become sensitized to His overwhelming love for us. Often it is during such times that we hear and begin to understand the secrets of Heaven.

***

Prayer: Father, reveal to me the wisdom, power and beauty of silence. I want to be attentive to hear Your heartbeat and Your still, small voice. It is Your whisper that I love, oh Lord, and Your secrets are my delight. Right now I take time to sit before You in silence, for You alone are worthy. You alone have the words of eternal life.

Day 4

Hebrews 11:6

He who comes to God must believe that He is and that He is a rewarder of those who diligently seek Him.

Faith empowers us to continually press in to know intimately the Christ who dwells within us. We believe that not only is He living within us, but that He has invited us to come and find Him there. In John 17 Jesus prayed to the Father that we would be with Him where He is, and that we would behold His beauty there. There is no place to "get to" in contemplative prayer, for He is already there. He is within us, waiting to meet with us in that place. *When we have this internal vision of Christ we will no longer attempt to get Him to come to us, nor will we strive in agitation to get to Him; rather, we will simply meet Him where He is.* Faith sustains a devotional life of beholding even during times of dryness, times when it feels like the Lord is hiding from us. Jesus orchestrates seasons of manifestation and seasons of hiddenness in our spiritual journey. He does this to increase our hunger and our thirst for Him alone. With divine purpose and with great care and perfect wisdom, He initiates such seasons. As we embrace the seasons that we are in He will be faithful to perfect love in us. Our job is to simply receive His great love and respond by giving Him our whole hearts in return. Our reward can be as profound as having our heart enlarged and having His divine nature released within us, or as simple as caring for our daily food.

Prayer: Father, help me to embrace the divine season You have placed me in. In times when You seem distant I will trust Your promise that You will never leave me or forsake me. You always show Yourself faithful. Thank You that in these times of hiddenness You are accomplishing that which will carry an eternal weight of glory. I come to You, Lord, knowing that You always do abundantly more than I could ever ask or think!

Day 5

Hebrews 12:2

Looking unto Jesus, the author and finisher of our faith...

Why would the writer to the Hebrews place this passage right after the Great Faith chapter of Hebrews eleven? It is as if the writer is saying, "You too can experience the faith of the great men and women listed here, but know assuredly that such faith comes only as you look to Jesus as the originator and finisher." The last verse of Romans chapter eleven proclaims that all things come from Jesus, through Jesus and back to Jesus. It's all about Jesus! I love the testimonies found in chapter 11 of Hebrews; seas split in two, lion's mouths being shut, and dead being raised... all by faith! Have you ever wondered why verse 21 was added to this great chapter? It simply says, "By faith Jacob, when he was dying, blessed each of the sons of Joseph, and worshiped, leaning on the top of his staff." No great healing or raising of the dead here, yet possibly the most beautiful and powerful of all the testimonies! Why was Jacob leaning on a staff? Genesis 32:28 gives us the story of Jacob wrestling with God until God dislocated Jacob's hip. The Lord says to Jacob, "Since you have prevailed ..." It sure looks to me like Jacob lost that wrestling match! Yet, we prevail with God as we allow him to shatter our own strength and self-sufficiency. At the end of Jacob's life he became a leaning lover, blessing the next generation. What a great picture of one leaning on the cross with no strength or wit of trickery left, only a heart to pour out to Jesus—and to the next generation!

Prayer: Father, help us to keep our eyes fixed on Jesus, the author and finisher of our faith. May we be a people who become limping, leaning lovers of Jesus. A people dependent on You, wholly trusting in Your kindness and faithfulness to work great exploits of faith for Your glory and honor. May You turn our hearts toward the coming generation in this hour, dear Lord.

Day 6

Hebrews 4:11

Labor to enter into rest.

To the undiscerning it may appear that the author of the book of Hebrews was having a "dumb moment" as this passage was being written. Certainly this passage contains divine wisdom and inspiration, yet it seems to be hiding in a paradox. This sounds like such a contradiction: labor to come into rest? Yet, there *is* a labor that brings us into rest, and it is against the soulish nature. There is a fight, a labor, a battle that we must engage in to resist the strength of the soul. It is natural to our human soul to live in an agitated state. To be anxious and bothered by many things is the result of a life empowered by the soul. Turning away from the carnal mind takes place as the Spirit draws us into rest. Due to the fact that the soul has empowered most Christians for most of their lives, it will take time and labor to resist its movements and learn to be led by the Spirit. When we know—when we truly know—the reality and the power of the Indwelling Christ, at this moment we begin our journey out of our soul's power and into union empowered by the Christ Life. At this point we will no longer need to submit to the soul's influence and its demands, we will begin to experience true rest. Christ is calling us today, saying, "All you who are weary and heavy laden, all you who are tired of being empowered by your soul, come unto Me and I will give you rest." For Christ is our rest, and in Him, within each of us, is a place where fear and anxiety cannot and do not exist. Let us labor to find this secret place.

Prayer: Father, bring us into the place of rest where no anxious thoughts or fear can inhabit. We thank You that in this life You have provided such a place within the depths of each Believer. Take us on this journey out of our soulish strength and into Your divine rest. Empower us to go into the depths of perfect love and union with the Indwelling Christ.

Day 7

1 Corinthians 1:30

But of Him you are in Christ Jesus, who became for us wisdom from God—and righteousness and sanctification and redemption... He who glories, let him glory in the Lord.

In the verses preceding this, Paul spoke clearly to the Corinthians that their human wisdom, their earthly position and even their nobility of birth were all equally unimpressive to God. Paul goes on to say that God chooses the foolish to shame the wise and the weak to confound the mighty. What, then, is the answer for a "successful" Christian life? God kept it a secret for ages, hidden in His heart of wisdom. He allowed many generations to try and attain righteousness and prove their godliness through their human strength and effort. Yet, this only confirmed their utter inability to do so. He did not allow this secret to be hidden for all times, though. This secret is the great mystery of the gospel: Christ in us, the hope of glory! The secret to successful Christianity is ever so simple and ever so profound. It is the life of the Vine that produces the fruit on the branches. We have been brought into a fellowship and a union with Christ, so that Christ in us can be Christ through us! We see in the above verse that we were put into Christ. *Christ in us is our only hope of true spirituality and power. Union with the Indwelling Christ is the secret of the ages that causes us to walk in victory.* Above everything else, beloved, let us come to a realization and a revelation that Christ in us is our answer. This is the great secret—the greatest of divine wisdom—now revealed!

Prayer: Father, bring us into union with the Indwelling Christ. May we find our nourishment and life from the True Vine. Unveil to us the power and the beauty of this glorious indwelling so that we can walk in the fullness of Christ and be perfected in the love of Christ.

Day 8

1 John 2:17

And the world is passing away, and the lust of it; but he who does the will of God abides forever.

What is God asking you to bring before Him that He might consume it in His jealous fire of love? He is always calling us to greater abandonment from things without and within. Only as these temporal distractions are given to Him can we give our hearts to Him with undivided devotion. As we sit before the Lord He will be faithful to reveal the inward, often unperceived attachments that subtly quench our first love. Let us allow the light of His gaze to reveal both the fear of man within and the love of earthly praise without. He will be faithful to bring us into fearless love as we sit in His presence and bring every earthly attachment to lay at His feet. Jesus asks—no, rather, he requires—an undivided love, for our hearts are not to be shared or divided among lesser loves. Only as we gaze on Jesus with singleness of eyes will first love be multiplied and poured out in us—and then through us to others. To this one, the overflow of first love will be a sweet fragrance both to our Heavenly Father and to those with whom we come in contact.

Prayer: Father, forgive me for giving myself to lust, pride and greed. These things do not exist in Heaven and will only be a distant memory there. Establish eternity in my heart as a compass and governor to lead me to the inner chambers of union. Empower me to live a life worthy of the calling of Christ—a life given to sitting at Your feet and then going from that place, clothed in Your life, to touch others.

Day 9

1 Peter 5:5-6

Be submissive to one another and be clothed with humility. Therefore humble yourself under the mighty hand of God that He may exalt you in due time.

Somebody once said, "Humility is a virtue all preach, none practice; and yet everybody is content to hear!" Certainly this statement is an exaggeration, and yet it is often more true than false. Over 300 years ago Francois Fenelon wrote about a false humility, which masqueraded in religious garments to hide a spirit of unbelief. He wrote, "There is a false humility which, acknowledging itself unworthy of the gifts of God, dares not confidently expect them. True humility consists in a deep view of our utter unworthiness, and in an absolute abandonment to God, without the slightest doubt that He will do great things for us."

The difference between false humility and true humility is often hidden to the undiscerning. False humility agrees that it is nothing, yet it does not progress into what true humility is. True humility acknowledges that it is nothing, yet lives with the profound and abiding understanding that we can do all things through Christ. Yes, we are nothing, but *in Him* we possess all things! It is only as we yield to the Indwelling One, who alone is truly humble, that we become clothed with His humility. The apostle Paul understood this. He said, "I know that in my flesh dwells no good thing." But on the other hand, he proclaimed, "It is Christ who lives in me who is my very life." Paul is one who walked in true humility, yet he also walked in great power and authority knowing it was Christ who worked His works through him!

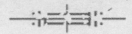

Prayer: *Father, thank You for making Jesus unto us not only wisdom, righteousness, sanctification and redemption, but humility as well. We come to You, Lord Jesus, to be clothed with Your life and true humility. It is You alone who has the absolute authority to abase those who exalt themselves and exalt those who walk in genuine humility. Empower us with Your grace, dear Lord, that we also would find the place of Your feet glorious!*

Day 10

2 Corinthians 3:18

But we all, with unveiled face, beholding as in a mirror the glory of the Lord, are being transformed into the same image from glory to glory, just as by the Spirit of the Lord.

Have you ever been told to simply quit sinning and straighten out your life? Quit lusting, quit being angry, and the list goes on. In an attempt to comply many have memorized scripture on holiness only to find their victories short-lived. Too often we have done a disservice to new converts by focusing on their weaknesses and vices. We have missed the heart of the gospel by trying to help them fight sin in the power of their dedication and consecration. Yet, there is a place of transformation at the feet of Jesus that does not require the energy of our own flesh.

This verse in Second Corinthians is utterly amazing. We simply behold as in a mirror the glory of the Lord—and we are transformed! We see in First Corinthians 13 that this mirror, or glass Paul speaks of, gives us only a dim reflection. The "mirror" of the New Testament times cannot be compared to the perfect reflection of modern mirrors. Have you ever been to a highway rest stop and found the bathroom mirror to be a piece of shiny metal? You strain to make out your reflection but the details are blurry. Yet, with even such a dim and vague beholding as this, the Scripture says we are changed from glory to glory. Paul is saying you don't have to be good at this, you don't even need to see clearly, just put yourself before the Lord and gaze upon Him and He will transform you. What a glorious promise! Do you want to be free from anger, from lust, from jealousy and insecurities? When we gaze on the ever-patient One we receive His very nature. When we gaze on the pure One our lust loosens its grip and its power. Seen from this vantage point, the Gospel is not so much about striving to be

82

like Jesus, but it becomes all about allowing Him to live His life through weak, broken people.

———— ⁛≡⁛≡⁛ ————

Prayer: *Father, in weakness I sit at the feet of Your Son Jesus and behold His glory. Thank You for the transformation that takes place even when I feel little or nothing of Your presence! It's all about You, Lord Jesus. May You be my very Life!*

Day 11

Isaiah 45:3

I will give you the treasures of darkness and the hidden riches of secret places, that you may know that I, the Lord, who call you by your name, am the God of Israel.

There is one treasure to be sought above all other treasures. This treasure is beyond worth to the Father who sits on the throne. It is reserved for those who sell everything to buy the field where this treasure can be found. When the treasure is found, God has provided that the seeker and the treasure form an eternal union.

Jesus Himself is this hidden treasure, buried in the field of the hearts of the redeemed. He remains hidden to the casual seeker, yet longs to be found, longs to be revealed to those who come to Him with their whole hearts. There are depths to the Man Christ Jesus that are reserved for those who have eyes for only Him. The eyes of our heart were given to us so that we might behold Him, that we would be transformed from glory to glory. This great transforming glory culminates in union with the Desire of the Nations, Jesus!

Prayer: *Father, reveal the beauty of Your Son to me so that I can be empowered to give myself fully to Him. Unveil the glorious Man Christ Jesus to Your Bride in this hour. Grace me, Lord, to seek You with utter abandonment, with a soft, open and passionate heart.*

Day 12

Isaiah 55:1-2

Everyone who is thirsty come to the waters; and you who have no money, come, buy and eat. Yes, come buy wine and milk without money and without cost... Listen carefully to Me and eat what is good and delight yourself in abundance.

What an incredible invitation! We see a similar invitation in Jesus' passionate proclamation found in John 7:37, "If any man is thirsty let him come to Me and drink."

God opens wide the door of His heart to everyone who would respond to such a glorious invitation. First He puts within us a thirst for Himself alone, a void that only can be permanently filled and satisfied with His great love. What joy it brings to His heart as we respond to this invitation! All He asks is that we bring our poor and needy hearts to Him, acknowledging that He alone is the Love that our hearts long for. Have you found any earthly lusts that satisfy and quench your hungry soul? These earthly imposters only bring us to ruin and despair. Yet, there is One, and only One, who can fascinate us; only One who has the power to fulfill and consummate the longings we sometimes cannot even identify. Isaiah 4:2 proclaims that in this hour, in this day, the Branch of the Lord shall be beautiful and glorious. This is our inheritance, Jesus alone will be made beautiful and glorious and take us as His very own!

Prayer: Lord Jesus, You alone are the beautiful and glorious one, You alone are eternal life. Christ, You are our very life. To drink of Your divine presence is the longing of my soul. Draw me to the deep place, that inward place where I can meet with You, draw me to that innermost place where rivers of living water flow! This is my cry and my desire, oh Lord.

Day 13

Isaiah 64:4

Men have not heard nor perceived by the ear, nor has the eye seen any god besides You, who acts for the one who waits for Him.

A literal translation of this verse could be, "...He who acts on behalf of those who wait on Him." This verse has become most precious to me the past few years as I have come to understand a glimpse of the glory and power of this promise.

Several years ago I was waiting on the Lord with a group of friends; we had formed a group to come together to wait in extended times of silence on the Lord, simply to be loved and love Him in return. We call these "corporate beholding times," and we have found them to be some of our favorite times with one another. During one of these gatherings we had waited on the Lord for about an hour, simply in silent adoration. As we began to share our time together one of the guys with great excitement shared what the Lord had spoken to him during this time. He said the Lord told him we had just been interceding for a specific city in eastern Israel. My first reaction was, "No we didn't—we were just loving Jesus. We were not interceding..."

In the next couple days I sought out the wisdom of my 90-year-old friend who has spent over 60 years in daily silence before the Lord. With great confidence, and countless experiences, he shared with me this verse in Isaiah and how the Lord will act and accomplish His will as He finds a people who will wait on Him. Wow! It is exciting to think that in our utter weakness and silence before the Lord He would be moving in His great wisdom and power.

Since that time we have shared many testimonies where the Lord has allowed us to glance into His workings during our times of waiting. There is never a time that is wasted in waiting in silence before Him. He is ever working in such times, whether there be a great manifestation of His presence or whether the time was full of distractions. It no longer matters whether we feel His presence or whether He seems miles away. We know that He is both willing and working his good pleasure in us and through us as we sit at His feet!

Prayer: *Father, we thank You for this promise in Isaiah that You act on behalf of those who wait on You. Thank You that You are always working in us and through us—even in times when we feel nothing!*

Day 14

Job 28:7, 8, 12, 13

There is a path no ravenous bird knows; nor has the eye of the hawk or vulture seen; ravenous beasts have not trodden it; nor has the fierce lion passed over it... Where can wisdom be found and where is the place of understanding?

God does not leave us as orphans to find our own way with our own strength. He does not leave us in the wilderness on the way to His house of many mansions. There is a less-frequented path that has been lost to busy generations. It appears lonely and forsaken to the eyes of the undiscerning, yet this inner path leads to Him who is Wisdom and in whom is found understanding.

There is a secret place where the Most High is our dwelling. It is a place where no evil can befall us and no plague can come near our abiding (Ps. 91:9-10). It is a secret place because the enemy does not know where it is, nor can he visit us there. It is the place within each of us where Jesus has made His abode. Have you heard of this inner mansion that was frequented by the mystics of old? Today there is a resurgence of hunger to return to this inner sanctum that Christ died to purchase. If the Lord is drawing you to this inner place where He abides, be ready to turn within. Gently position your heart to be loved and to simply love in return. This is the beginning of the journey of all journeys—the journey within!

Prayer: Thank You, Lord Jesus, for preparing a place within the very center of my being where we can meet. Open my inner eyes to see the glory of this secret place. Take me away from external distractions and help me to nurture this interior life.

Day 15

John 12:3

Mary therefore took a pound of very costly perfume of pure nard, and anointed the feet of Jesus, and wiped His feet with her hair; and the house was filled with the fragrance of the perfume.

Mary, who could usually be found at the feet of Jesus, is at His feet once again pouring out her heart before her lover and Lord. The tender compassion of Jesus had captured Mary's whole heart and she knew that there were no words she could speak that could ever be enough to communicate her love and gratitude. Her love must be poured out—costly, extravagant and fragrant—she would give all that she had.

There are several passages in Scripture where we find people falling at the feet of Jesus to petition Him with their requests. It was Mary who fell at His feet with no other intention than simply to give Him her whole heart. It was an inward reality of extravagant love poured out in this external act. Why did Jesus declare that wherever the Gospel would be preached this testimony of Mary would also be proclaimed? Could it be that this same heart of devotion is what the Gospel produces wherever it is proclaimed? It is forever a memorial to all the ages crying out, "He is worth everything, for He *is* everything!" The life that Mary lived invites us into the same reality. If we will sit and gaze upon our Beloved, we too will go from glory to glory and His fragrance will emanate from us, His Bride.

Prayer: Lord Jesus, draw me into the reality of this love. Only You, Love itself, can cause my weak heart to love with such devotion, with such abandonment. Thank You that it was You who placed in my heart this longing for You. Knowing this, I have utter confidence that You will answer my cries and that my testimony will be that of the goodness of God. Thank You for pouring the fragrance of Christ upon Your Bride in this hour.

Day 16

John 12:24

Jesus said, "Unless a grain of wheat falls into the ground and dies, it remains alone; but if it dies, it produces much fruit."

Have you ever received a wonderful word of promise from the Lord only to find your life going in the opposite direction? Did you go from the mountaintop of expectancy to the valley of contradiction, crushing, and even despair? The time between receiving a promise from God and its fulfillment is called the valley of contradiction and crisis. There is a secret to spiritual maturity: accomplishment in the spirit realm is directly proportionate to the crucifixion of our self-life so that Christ may live unhindered through us.

In this hour the Lord is leading His people to greater spiritual power and authority. Yet, great prayers and great promises always demand great preparation. During such contradictions in our lives we must not let our hearts be troubled, for He who began a good work in us will certainly finish it. There are degrees of fruitfulness; some thirty, some sixty and some one-hundredfold. In each progression of fruitfulness there is a progression of a deeper death to the workings of the self-life. As we fall into this death and die, the very life of Christ begins to grow and flow more abundantly through us.

When the Lord was preparing Joseph for leadership he "buried" him in slavery, prison and a foreign land for 20 years. When God was preparing Moses for his leadership God "buried" him in the backside of a desert for 40 years. When Saul of Tarsus had the meeting on the road to Damascus, God "buried" him in the wilderness of Arabia for many years. If we are asking God to make us abundantly fruitful we can be sure that we will first fall to the ground and die. God doesn't delight in our suffering, but in our purification and in our transformation.

———⋰⋰=⟨⟩⋰⋰———

Prayer: *Father, help me to embrace the bitter north winds as they come to root out the self-life. Thank You, Lord, that You do not leave me desolate in the wilderness, but that You give me enough grace for each day. May my life and testimony bring glory to Your name as I embrace the contradictions and wait for the deliverance that only You can bring.*

Day 17

John 14:23

Jesus answered and said to him, "If anyone loves Me, he will keep My Word; and My Father will love him, and We will come to him and make Our abode with him."

In the context of this passage, Jesus is preparing His disciples for His departure. He comforts them with words of promise, "I will not leave you as orphans." In this next phase of ministry, Jesus proclaims the great mystery of His indwelling presence in each Believer. He assures them that this transition will be better for them.

Within each of us, there is a secret place where we can go and hide in Him. In this aiding place we can behold His glory, and it is in this place that He discloses Himself to us. My 90-year old friend who has sat at the feet of Jesus for more than 60 years has told me often, "Chris, your fight will always be to sit at the feet of Jesus; everything and everybody will pull you from this place, but hold your ground for it is in this place that He may be found in great simplicity and, yet, in great glory."

Prayer: Lord Jesus, although I do not see You with my natural eye, the eyes of my heart behold Your beauty and cause me to love You more with each gaze. May the unseen realm be more real to me than that which I can behold with my physical senses. Thank You for Your precious indwelling. I pray You would continue to bring me deeper and deeper into the depths of Your life. Bring me into union with You as I travel through the interior castle of Your presence.

Day 18

John 15:5

I am the vine, you are the branches. He who abides in Me, and I in him, bears much fruit; for without Me you can do nothing.

Blessed is the one who is brought into the realization that apart from Christ he can do nothing. Why is this awareness such a rare attainment in this hour? This might be one of the most difficult lessons a human being can learn in this life. We are told from an early age that we can accomplish anything if we would only put our mind to it. Our lives are often centered on reaching a place of popularity, power and prestige. Have you entered into a season in your Christian walk where you find you can no longer do something well which you have been doing well your whole life? Maybe you were able to pray and intercede for extended periods of time, or you were one who could easily hear the Lord's voice. Yet now you find words fumbling out at your prayer times, or you are having a difficult time hearing the Lord like you once did. Or, now when a fast is called, you are unable to find the strength to make it through the first day, let alone the first meal.

Well I have good news for you! The Lord has withdrawn his empowerment from your soulish disciplines to show you that apart from Him you have no strength. Are these perplexing times? Difficult seasons? It can be very painful to discover our utter helplessness. How blessed is the person who finds out he can do nothing of himself; it is even more glorious when we even stop attempting to do anything in our own strength. It is at this point we begin to glorify the Lord in a new and powerful way. With this revelation we begin a journey into His Life and His leading whereby He governs all of our movements. This awareness of our poverty is one of the most precious gifts given to man (Matt. 5:3). Now instead of trying to fast or trying to pray, we enter into His invitation to fast, and pray with His strength empowering us!

Prayer: *Father, help me to embrace my utter inability to accomplish anything using my own strength. Empower me, oh Lord, to stop attempting to "try" to do anything apart from Your leading and Your Life. May poverty of spirit and purity of heart mark my life, and may the living Christ move powerfully through my weakness!*

Day 19

John 4:13-14

Jesus answered and said to her, "Whoever drinks of this water shall thirst again, but whoever drinks of the water that I shall give him shall never thirst; but the water that I shall give him will become in him a well of water springing up to everlasting life."

The Father beautifully orchestrates this encounter between Jesus and this thirsty woman. Jesus reveals to her that her outward thirst is a heightened expression of an inward thirst for reality, for life-giving water. Jesus' presence and words only create in her a more desperate thirst—an awareness of her need to be satisfied with something of eternity. He speaks to her of a well that will indwell those who believe on Him. This well will be the very life of God indwelling His followers so that they can intimately commune and continuously partake of the Living Water, Christ Himself.

God wants His children to know experientially how deep and satisfying His Life within them can be. There is a satisfying draught of divine life given to those who learn to fellowship with the indwelling Christ. This living water causes the human heart to fully surrender and deeply love the Lord Jesus. As our hearts encounter Him as the "lover of our soul" we will respond with extravagant love.

Prayer: *Father, I need a greater revelation of this river of life that runs deep within. My heart yearns to drink deeply of this Eternal Fountain, Jesus Himself. Jesus, teach me the power and the beauty of drinking from Your divine indwelling presence.*

Day 20

Luke 24:13, 27, 32

Now behold, two of them were traveling that same day to a village called Emmaus... And beginning at Moses and all the Prophets He expounded to them in all the Scriptures the things concerning Himself... "Did not our hearts burn within us as He talked with us... and opened the Scriptures to us?"

Have you ever wondered why Jesus would spend an entire day walking with two men, opening up every book of the Bible concerning Himself? Certainly this was the greatest sermon ever preached. The topic was Jesus, the text was the whole Word of God, and the preacher was Christ Himself. Wow! I can't believe it was not caught on tape or at least hand written for us to enjoy forever! No, Jesus "wasted" this incredible sermon on two men! Why would He do such a thing? Certainly He is not teasing the rest of us with this story, making our mouths water for such an encounter only to say, "Sorry, it's for these two and not you!"

I think what He is communicating is this: wherever and whenever He finds a person who will give Him their undistracted devotion, listening to Him intently, He will do the same thing with them. He longs to reveal Himself to the soul that gives Him time. This story is meant to encourage us. There was no need to write this sermon down, for He desires to give it afresh, day after day to those who are willing to walk with Him and wait upon Him! As we walk with Him in abandonment we will enjoy the delight of a burning heart. When our hearts burn in this manner our only thought is how we can please our beloved Lord and love Him more.

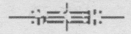

Prayer: Lord Jesus, I desire to walk with You on the Emmaus Road of my own heart so You would reveal to me the beauty of who You are. Thank You, Lord, for Your willingness and Your passionate desire to be known by mere humans. Oh how our hearts long to spend undistracted time in Your presence, sharing intimate secrets as friends. Burn our hearts, oh Lord, with Your divine love.

Day 21

Mark 1:35

Now in the morning, having risen a long while before daylight, [Jesus] went out and departed to a solitary place; and there He prayed.

The previous night the whole city of Galilee had gathered at His door, many of whom were healed and delivered. Surely the next morning Jesus was tired in His body, yet He knew His need to find a solitary place to be with His Father. In this quiet place the refreshing and empowering of divine life and divine love would flow through Him.

The life of Jesus was sustained through intimacy and union with the Father. Jesus had emptied Himself and was made in the likeness of man: in order for Him to bear fruit on the Earth, He would have to keep His Father's commandments and abide in His love. Certainly Jesus would never expect us to live in a manner in which He had not first walked. He continually and habitually would slip away to be alone with the Father for times of undistracted intimacy and prayer.

Prayer: Lord Jesus, I want to abide in Your love. Draw me into fellowship and prayer continually. I look to You to lead me into a life of deep prayer. May I never get so caught up in ministry and business that I forget that my daily empowering comes from Your indwelling life. Grace me, Lord, to set times throughout the day to pull away with You, my Lord and my Friend.

Day 22

Mark 15:3-5

And the chief priest accused Him of many things, but He answered nothing. Then Pilate asked Him again, saying, "Do you answer nothing? See how many things they testify against You!" But Jesus still answered nothing, so that Pilate marveled.

The Gospel records a handful of times when men and women marveled at Jesus. One passage says, "What manner of man is this, that even the winds and the sea obey him!" People marveled at His wisdom in responding to the Pharisees' trick questions. They marveled at His authority over nature, over demons and even over the cursing of a fig tree. Now they are marveling over His silence! Was Jesus out of words? Did He not know how to respond to the accusations against Him? Could He not justify Himself? He kept His silence at all the spiteful disrespect of ignorant men.

Often due to the state of our hearts we feel the need to answer our critics and respond to those who would seek our downfall. Too often we answer back with arrogance and justifications at those who accuse us, while all along the Lord wants to purge us from self-love and self-preservation. Sometimes when we defend ourselves and answer back we miss the opportunity to walk as Jesus walked, and to allow His beauty to be seen upon us. Speaking quickly in our own defense in times of adversity or accusation blocks His life from being seen through us. Could this be a way we rob the Lord of His glory? The Lord is patiently teaching us little by little that our own strength will never bring the rule and reign of Christ into our hearts, homes and cities.

Prayer: Lord Jesus, may I know when to speak and when to hold my peace!

Day 23

Numbers 14:24

...My servant Caleb, because he has a different spirit in him and has followed Me fully...

Caleb's spirit stood out from those around him. Caleb had a spirit that was taken up with God. He was jealous for the will of God and he trusted in the power and faithfulness of the Almighty. Those around him were fleshy, frightened and without honor. Their sight could only reach as high as the giants of Anak. Yet Caleb could see beyond these warriors to the Great Warrior! In Psalm two we see that God sits in the heavens and laughs at those who stand against Him and against His Anointed. The Lord is looking in this hour for a people who are not divided, not half-hearted concerning His purposes and call, but rather who have a "different" spirit, a spirit like Caleb. The beloved John in his first epistle writes, "...He who is in you is greater than he who is in the world." Have you found the indwelling Christ to be greater than your circumstances, greater than the problems and fears arrayed against you? If we would take time to turn within to behold the beauty and majesty of Christ, we too would become a people with a "different" spirit. Spiritual warfare is not so much about attacking the enemy as it is about seeing the glory and majesty of the indwelling Christ. When we see Him, we begin to see the enemies of the Lord as they really are. The tables turn and God's enemies are seen as "grasshoppers" in comparison to *Him*!

Prayer: God, by Your grace we will not fear our enemies, but we will rise up in the Might of Him who dwells within, overcoming all that is arrayed against us. Grace us to live with eternity in our hearts and vision that looks beyond the natural into the supernatural. Thank You for making us into a people with a "different" spirit!

Day 24

Philippians 2:12-13

Therefore, my beloved, as you have always obeyed, not in my presence only, but now much more in my absence, work out your own salvation with fear and trembling. For it is God who works in you both to will and to do for His good pleasure.

Paul is making an appeal for obedience; not an obedience that is revealed only when we are seen, but an obedience that is deeply rooted and grounded so as to produce a secret obedience through our relationship with the One who indwells us. This passage is not presenting a new way of salvation based on good works. Instead it is saying, in effect, that we are completely helpless and unable to make ourselves better or bring about any good works apart from God who works in us. Yet, as God initiates His working within us, there is a response He must have from us. We must yield to Him through faith and obedience to His inner workings. We are not under a code of laws in self-motivated obedience, but rather we are placing ourselves under the headship of our indwelling Savior; we are walking in faith and obedience to Christ within. As we do this He can express His nature and His life through us. What an incredible promise! He both *wills in us* and *does in us* His good pleasure as we yield to this inward working.

Prayer: Lord, we ask for a spirit of full obedience to You inner voice, the inner working of Your presence. Lord, help us to be attentive to this still, small voice that we would sense and know both Your will and the energizing power within to perform that will. May we walk as You walk and do the works that You have done, for it is Your glory both to will and to work in us for Your good pleasure!

Day 25

Philippians 3:8-9

I also count all things loss for the excellence of the knowledge of Christ Jesus my Lord, for whom I have suffered the loss of all things, and count them as rubbish, that I may gain Christ and be found in Him.

This is no sterile cry for a legal or positional standing in Christ. Paul had a deep longing in his heart, an almost indescribable passion to remain in unbroken union and fellowship with Christ. Paul understood that to live godly in Christ Jesus would cause him great persecution. We are reminded when Paul preached in Lystra, he was stoned, left for dead, and dragged out of the city, only to awaken hours later and walk back in the same city! Who was this man? Certainly he was a spectacle to men and women, and even to angels, of an extravagant, unearthly love. He wasn't asking to be excused from trials and persecutions, nor was he asking for them. He was only concerned that in all things he be found in Christ. Paul knew that his only refuge and safety from defeats and discouragements was a moment-by-moment union with the Indwelling Savior.

I recently came across a story about Francois Fenelon, the Archbishop of Cambrai in the 1600's. In this story, Fenelon was at ease in a pleasant conversation with a group of people. Suddenly a friend interrupted him, saying that a fire had burned down the archiepiscopal palace and consumed all Feneolon's books, along with his personal writings. Fenelon interrupted his friend and assured him that he had already been informed, and that yes, it was a great loss. However, Fenelon went on to say, "I would rather have my library burn down than some poor peasant's cottage." He had just lost years of writings and thousands of dollars in books and manuscripts, yet Fenelon was found *in Christ*. The man that discipled Graham Cooke told him, "There are no more good days or bad days, only days of grace. Grace to enjoy what is happening or grace to endure what is happening." This is the testimony of those who are found in Christ!

Prayer: Father, I desire to be found in Christ no matter what the trial or circumstance that You allow in my life. Empower me, dear Lord, to live in that place of unbroken fellowship and union. Help me to live honorably both in service and in secret, I pray!

Day 26

Psalm 34:8

Oh taste and see that the Lord is good.

The human heart has been created to experience God. This heart has the God-given capacity to intimately know, to love, to worship and to respond to God. The heart has the ability to commune with God in a way that is both personal and experiential.

The psalmist declares with a passionate invitation, "Taste the goodness of God! See the goodness of God!" Let this revelation and understanding of His nature overwhelm you. It is not enough to hear about His goodness towards Moses, Elijah or even your neighbor or spouse! God wants each of us to have our own life rooted and grounded in His goodness and His love. It is His desire to pour His goodness into our hearts. He will give each of us our very own testimony of who God is *to us*!

We are promised in Psalm 27 that if we wait on the Lord we will see His goodness in the land of the living. So let your heart take courage and wait on the Lord. For if we do this, our testimony will be, "He is *good!*"

Prayer: *Lord Jesus, I want to know Your goodness. I want to be firmly rooted in the understanding of how great Your goodness is towards me. I know that a revelation of Your goodness and love will cause my heart to be unshakable in times of testing and pain. Help me to wait on You in faith, believing that goodness will surely follow me all the days of my life.*

Day 27

Psalm 46:10

Be still and know that I am God.

Deep intimacy with God cannot be fully entered into without learning to quiet our soul in His presence. An inner atmosphere of stillness is essential to experiencing deep communing love with the Indwelling Christ. How else shall we hear that "still, small voice" if we have not learned through patience and love to silence our own inward clamoring? It is through patience and love that this is learned. We simply, gently, and continually turn our heart to Him, while His love and beauty draws our heart into His presence. Do not be discouraged if during such times your mind wanders to thoughts of paying bills, phone calls you need to make, or any of a thousand other distractions. For He is pleased to go with us in the distraction and help us re-gather our thoughts back on Him.

Is this great prize of finding His indwelling presence worth it if it takes us a week, a month or even a year to silence the inner noises? Certainly for such a great treasure as finding and abiding in the Indwelling Christ we can persevere and enjoy the entire process, both the difficult and the refreshing times. To Jesus the process is as important as the destination, for He is in both and thus He can be glorified in both! As we are faithful and patient we will discover that God is at work within us and that our inward life is enlarging.

Prayer: *Lord Jesus, I long to be completely at rest in You, to have my soul quieted and composed, like a child resting in the arms of its father. Your marvelous ways cause me to sit before You in silent wonder. Thank You, Lord, for inviting me into the secret place so that my heart can live in unbroken fellowship with You.*

Day 28

Psalm 45:13-14

The royal daughter is all glorious within; her clothing is woven with gold. She shall be brought to the King in robes of many colors; the virgins, her companions who follow her, shall be brought to Thee.

True godliness is wrought from within by God Himself. As we abandon ourselves to Him and spend time being loved and loving Him in return, His nature will grow deep within us. The King's daughter is glorious within because she has nurtured her interior life. She diligently guarded this place where she carried the life of God. She did not let the little foxes spoil love as she tended her vineyard. As she responded to His love with great abandonment, He wove the golden thread and produced the character of Christ in her. She allowed this process to take place with every response of her heart toward Him. She was led into His innermost chamber, the "glorious within." It is His careful love that does this work of beautiful embroidery, leading us into deeper love and abandonment. The embroidery at times may be painful and the gold only becomes pure through the fires of testing. Yet, to those who embrace such contradictions, the life and fragrance of Christ becomes so alluring and beautiful that others will want to follow and know this glorious Man, Christ Jesus!

Prayer: Lord Jesus, I love the way You faithfully and carefully change my heart from within. You overwhelm me, Lord, with the thought that You are actually forming Your very life within me. Your beauty is indescribable, and You clothe me with such beauty as this. You have responded to me with a kindness I have yet to comprehend, my words cannot express such thanksgiving, yet my heart resounds with the cry from within, "I love You! I love You, my Lord!"

Day 29

Psalm 62:5

My soul, wait in silence for God only, for my hope is from Him.

Those who have developed a life of waiting on God know that it is God alone who can meet the deep cries of the human heart. All hope is seemingly cut off and all seems lost until one leans on the breast of Jesus and hears the heartbeat of the One who is hope. How blessed is the person who has come to know that the fruit of the Spirit is not simply gifts in a box, but that this fruit is the person of Christ for us to receive. He is our hope; He is the love we so desperately desire. It is this revelation and understanding that enables the soul to wait in silence, resting in the goodness of God, knowing that He will answer in His wisdom and in His time.

A wise man once said, "What God allows in His wisdom, He could have easily prevented by His power." The soul that waits on the Lord rests in the understanding that God is wise enough to govern the lives of men and women, and His heart can be fully trusted. He is a God of infinite love, completely devoid of selfishness. His will for each one of us flows out of who He is, so it can only be good, perfect and acceptable. Sometimes it is the wisdom of God to allow testings and trials to come so He can root out of us everything that hinders love. When our hope is in Him and of Him, we will find rest in who He is.

Prayer: Lord Jesus, I long for my soul to wait before You in silence. At times I can only hear my own fear. During these times my soul feels so much turmoil that peace seems to elude me. Yet, I will find rest in You, confident that my life truly is in Your hands. I can fully trust Your great wisdom and mercy, even in times when Your manifest presence is hidden from me!

Day 30

Revelation 2:17

To him who overcomes I will give some of the hidden manna to eat.

In the holy place of the temple during Old Testament times, there was placed what was called "Presence-bread." It was made of the finest wheat, symbolizing Christ's perfect and pure humanity. This bread could not be removed from the holy place and could only be eaten by the priests in the temple. While the Presence-bread was a precious figure of Jesus Christ, it was only eaten once a week. In comparison, the manna of the Old Testament that was dropped from Heaven came as Israel's daily food from God. The Presence-bread was made by man and could only be kept for seven days, but the manna had no touch of human origin upon it. The Presence-bread wonderfully symbolized Jesus Christ as the life and nourishment of those who minister in the holy place. Yet, how much more glorious it is for us, New Testament kings and priests, to partake of the very Manna of Heaven, Christ Himself. There is a secret place within each one of us where we feed upon Jesus Christ as our Hidden Manna.

Prayer: Lord Jesus, we have eaten of the fruit of our own lusts and been unsatisfied and unfulfilled. Take us to the place of Your presence and feed us the hidden manna of Your very life. For we know, Lord Jesus, that only the Tree of Life, Christ Himself, can nourish and quench every hunger and thirst of the human soul.

CHAPTER III

Realms of Spiritual Living

Jill Austin

Jill Austin is a powerful prophetic voice with a catalytic anointing, moving in the manifest presence of God. Releasing the fires of Holy Spirit, she brings fresh passion and hunger for Jesus Christ as lives are transformed and people are challenged and equipped for the work of the Kingdom.

As the founder of Master Potter Ministries, Jill has traveled extensively for over 20 years as a national and international conference speaker, ministering the Gospel with signs and wonders following.

Jill ministers to leaders as well as the broader body of Christ, delivering prophetic proclamations and words that release impartation, unlocking their destinies and birthrights. Her pioneering spirit assists in bringing churches, cities and nations to a place of spiritual breakthrough.

For more information about hosting a Jill Austin conference or for a complete listing of available products, please e-mail her at info@masterpotter.com. We would also like to invite you to visit her website at www.masterpotter.com.

Day 1 – Apostolic Power: Pressing in for a New Pentecost

Acts 2:1-4

When the Day of Pentecost had fully come, they were all with one accord... and suddenly there came a sound from Heaven, as of a rushing mighty wind, and it filled the whole house where they were sitting. Then there appeared to them divided tongues, as of fire... and they were all filled with the Holy Spirit.

The Kingdom of God can only successfully invade the dominion of Satan when we are endued with power from on high. You must have spiritual power to advance the Kingdom.

How did they do it? Jesus warned the disciples of their need to wait and receive the power of the Holy Spirit: "Behold, I send the promise of My Father upon you; but tarry in the city of Jerusalem until you are endued with power from on high (Luke 24:49)." As they met in the upper room for ten days, their only agenda was to pray and wait on God. They knew that they must have more. They were not leaving with anything less!

Holy Spirit brings the government of God. What is often overlooked is that the Acts two outpouring was what *birthed* the early church. Holy Spirit is more than a phenomenon of fire and wind or just a renewal movement—*the third Person of the Trinity invaded the upper room to establish the Kingdom of God!*

Being baptized by the Holy Spirit was more than just speaking in tongues. The enemy has so religiously minimized this experience by convincing us that if we speak our five or ten words in tongues, then we have arrived. Unfortunately, often we still do not have apostolic power!

Holy Spirit is not just tongues. In Acts 2:8-11, He brought a miracle of languages with over fifteen languages being heard by the crowds. People heard the testimony of Jesus, but in their own native tongue.

The Great Commission for souls was birthed. The wind and fire of the Spirit drew a huge crowd who then heard Peter preach his first sermon. This holy tornado of the Spirit yielded 3,000 souls that day. For the first time, Peter was endued with power and moved in apostolic authority with the power of the Holy Spirit backing his words. Signs and wonders followed the apostles and churches spread like wildfire (Acts 2:41-47).

Do you want to walk in this fullness of apostolic authority? When you speak, does the power of conviction pierce hearts? How do we get this great outpouring of the Holy Spirit? We must have an even greater desperation. Today, the Lord is calling for another Pentecost! Imagine the power of Acts synergistically combined with the astonishing signs and wonders of Exodus! This is the hour we are approaching as we near the second coming of Christ. God is going to explode in an expression of power that we have never seen before! Are you desperate for a fresh baptism of fire from the Holy Spirit?

Prayer: *Lord, burn in me a holy desperation to move in apostolic authority with signs and wonders following. I want to move in the Holy Spirit and establish the government of God on this Earth!*

Day 2 – The Breaker Anointing

Micah 2:13

The one who breaks open will come up before them; they will break out, pass through the gate, and go out by it; their king will pass before them, with the Lord at their head.

What does it take for Heaven to invade Earth? It takes a breaker anointing! One of God's names in the Bible actually is the "Breaker." A breaker anointing is a catalytic deposit of the Holy Spirit where eternity breaks through into the natural realm. It is a holy invasion in which the gates of Heaven are opened!

This type of anointing will break through every obstacle and hindrance to the furtherance of the Gospel. It shakes every shackle loose that holds individuals and the Church back from coming into their destiny and inheritance. Jesus promises that "the Kingdom suffers violence and the violent take it by force (Matt. 11:12)." The breaker anointing is the core anointing for the advancement of the apostolic church.

Today there is tremendous warfare at the gates of our cities; there is a contesting at these gates to shut down the supernatural. Demonic forces often control the entry way of God's presence. For example, you may feel a tangible heaviness, a ceiling or oppression in a service. It takes a breaker anointing to open up the spiritual atmosphere so Heaven can invade Earth.

When the breaker anointing occupies an area, individuals, churches, socio-political structures and belief systems are revolutionized. The Breaker must come if we are to see the transformation of our cities.

Let me offer you one of my favorite examples of one who carried this anointing. Maria-Woodworth Etter was a healing evangelist in this past century. She was such a friend of Holy

Spirit (as you are learning to be) that for fifty miles around her, the glory of the Lord would cover that region. A glory cloud with a fifty-mile radius surrounded her with signs and wonders following!

Do you want a breaker anointing? Do you want the fullness of the Holy Spirit? The Lord wants to once again manifest Himself as the Breaker. Get ready! Cry out for this anointing!

Prayer: Lord, I am going to press into this because I am hungry for all of You. What I have is good, but it is not enough. I want my life to carry a breaker anointing. I want my life to break out to touch people who are suffering so that they can experience breakthroughs in their own lives. I want to contend at my city gates and bring Heaven to Earth!

Day 3 – Visitations: Key to City Transformation

Exodus 3:2-3, 16-17

And the Angel of the Lord appeared to him [Moses] in a flame of fire from the midst of a bush. He looked and behold, the bush was burning with fire, but the bush was not consumed. Then Moses said, "I will now turn aside and see this great sight, why the bush does not burn" ... Go and gather the elders of Israel together and say to them, "The Lord God of your fathers, the God of Abraham, of Isaac, and of Jacob, appeared to me, saying, 'I have surely visited you and seen what is done to you in Egypt; and I have said I will bring you up out of the affliction of Egypt to the land of the Canaanites... to a land flowing with milk and honey.'"

What empowered Moses to stand before Pharaoh and courageously declare "Let my people go?" One encounter with a burning bush and Moses was forever changed. Not only was Moses ruined for God, but this personal visitation was what emblazoned Moses to become the deliverer of a nation!

Do you want to see God change your city? The common question I hear in conferences across America is, "How do we bring in a revival? How do we bring Heaven to Earth? How do we welcome in the King of Glory?" I believe that one key to city transformation is personal visitation. For God to change your city, you must first have a radical visitation yourself. If you want to usher in a major move of God, you must first and foremost have an encounter with God yourself.

There is a misconception and lie in the Church that visitations are just for personal purposes where you have awesome adventures like riding in chariots of fire, eating on the Sapphire Sea like the Elders did with Moses, and playing with angels. But is that the only reason God gives us radical encounters with Him?

If we examine Scripture, we will see how the majority of our forefathers in the faith had a personal encounter with God to launch them into their destiny so that they could change the course of Biblical history. The result of these hallmark encounters were not just that they themselves were touched, but also that God's people were radically blessed. We cannot divorce city transformation from personal encounters with God. If you want revival, cry out for radical encounters with Jesus!

Prayer: Lord, I want a radical visitation from You! Just like You suddenly appeared to Moses, I ask for a holy ambush of Your Spirit. I ask that You would put a bullseye on my heart and ruin me for Jesus! I must have more! Use me like You used Moses to deliver an entire nation after just one personal encounter!

Day 4 – Revival and Revolution

Acts 19:8-10

And he [Paul] went into the synagogue and spoke boldly ... and this continued for two years, so that all who dwelt in Asia heard the word of the Lord Jesus, both Jews and Greeks.

1 Corinthians 2:5

And my speech and my preaching were not with persuasive words of human wisdom, but in demonstration of the Spirit and of power, that your faith should not be in the wisdom of men but in the power of God.

Acts 19 is the most outstanding success story of Paul's missionary career. One of the greatest triumphs of his life was that the entire province of Asia was evangelized in two years. The revival fire spread throughout all of Asia Minor and in 312 A.D., even brought about the conversion of Emperor Constantine. Christianity became the dominant religion in the Roman Empire, which had once tried to extinguish the early Church.

Can you imagine the Gospel spreading so quickly that even the pagan leaders of other countries would become radically saved? If it happened 2000 years ago, why not today? When there is a demonstration of the Holy Spirit's power, entire nations are transformed!

The government of God backed up Paul's words with such extraordinary signs and wonders that an entire continent was touched in only *two* years! Beloved, it will take more than just eloquent teaching to touch this generation. *We must have the power of God!* We need to cry out for a fresh baptism of fire—another Pentecost—if we want this magnitude of revival and revolution in our cities.

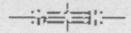

Prayer: *Oh Lord, I want to see Your glory touch this nation and spread to the ends of the Earth! I want the power of the Holy Spirit to invade my life, my city, my continent. If You would use Paul, why not use me? Today, Lord, I am asking You for a fresh baptism of fire from the Holy Spirit. I want the government of Your Kingdom to back up my words so that thousands will be saved.*

Day 5 – Taking the Prophetic to the Streets:
A Church Without Walls

Isaiah 61:1-2

The Spirit of the Lord God is upon Me, because the Lord has anointed Me to preach good tidings to the poor; He has sent Me to heal the brokenhearted; to proclaim liberty to the captives, the opening of the prison to those who are bound; to proclaim the acceptable year of the Lord, and the day of vengeance of our God; to comfort all who mourn.

I like to think of Isaiah 61 as the basic job description of all Believers. This is Christianity 101—*normal Christianity!* God wants the glory of the Lord to start to move in you and through you! How many of you would like to have hospitals close down in your region because of the signs, wonders and miracles exploding in your church and everyday life?

Perhaps your concept of evangelism is being part of a weekly team that hits the streets of an impoverished section of town, armed and ready with tracts. Maybe you mechanically pass out the Four Spiritual Laws to a common passerby with a simple, "Jesus loves you." In this hour could it be that passing out tracts is too limited and impersonal? Beloved, this is good, but it is only the beginning! God wants more for you! God desires all men to be saved and He wants to use *you!* He wants you to be a living tract. He wants to use your mouth to speak His words; your hands to stretch forth in signs and wonders; your feet to be carriers of the Good News.

Just as Jesus ministered to each person in the Gospels in a unique way, God wants us to learn to hear His heart for each individual and deliver the Gospel in a tailor-made package for them. For one person, it might be buying them a cup of coffee, another might receive a word of knowledge or a prophecy, or God might want you to heal someone in the grocery store. Whatever He says to do, we need to do it!

Jesus Christ had the keys to open up the gates of Hell and set the captives free. Now that He has redeemed us, He has put keys in our hands. We can touch the broken-hearted by unlocking secret doors of past history and family secrets to set them free.

God wants to explode out from the box that we call Church! He wants to catapult you into the marketplace as His hands, His heart and His feet. If you are waiting for someone else to do it, God says, "Guess what? You're it!"

Congratulations! You are His hand-picked brigade of fishermen! He wants to give you fishing nets. He has been healing the holes in your nets so that you can cast them into the dark seas of humanity. The shekinah glory will spread as it hits the water, and the fish will be drawn to it. When He is lifted up, all men draw near. Now is the hour to go fishing!

Prayer: *God, release Your Spirit. Teach us not only how to know Your message, but how to be Your message. Break our hearts for the lost. Teach us to cast our nets and use every opportunity to reel in the fish. Father, help us not to hoard Your goodness, but to proclaim that this is the year of the favor of the Lord to all who want to hear the Good News!*

Day 6 – Casting a Dangerous Shadow

Acts 5:15-16

... People brought the sick into the streets and laid them on the beds and mats so that at least Peter's shadow might fall on some of them as they passed by. Crowds gathered also from the towns around Jerusalem to bring their sick and those tormented by evil spirits and all of them were healed.

Is your shadow dangerous? In your arena of everyday life, do people get healed and delivered because so much of the resurrection power, the glory of the Lord, radiates through you? Is no one "safe" in your company because the Lord breaks in suddenly with visitations of deliverance, salvation and healing?

God wants people whose very name is known in Hell because they wreak such havoc on Satan's kingdom! We cannot bumble blindly through this world in mediocre, lukewarm lethargy. Peter carried so much authority that wherever his *shadow* fell, people were instantly healed. It wasn't Peter's own power—rather it was the glory of the Lord in Peter. Christ in you is the hope of glory!

When you walk into a restaurant, do you literally change the atmosphere because you carry so much of the fire of God in you? The Lord wants you to minister outside the walls of the church in everyday life to a hurt and dying world. Beloved, you are a carrier of His glory. Every place your hands and feet touch should be invaded with the resurrection power of God.

———————

Prayer: Oh Lord, I want to cast a dangerous shadow! Teach me to walk as a living flame so that all those around me are ignited with passion for You. So many are suffering today and I just want to let You radiate through me so that all will be saved. Teach me to be a carrier of Your glory.

Day 7 – Joshua's Journey: Are You a Giant-Killer?

Numbers 13:32-33

And they gave the children of Israel a bad report of the land which they had spied out, saying, "The land through which we have gone as spies is a land that devours its inhabitants, and all the people whom we saw in it are men of great stature. There we saw the giants (the descendants of Anak came from the giants); and we were like grasshoppers in our own sight, and so we were in their sight."

Are you the Moses generation or the Joshua generation? Moses sent men to spy out the Promised Land, and they returned with a bad report because of their fear of the giants. Instead of trusting the Lord, their hearts shriveled and they saw themselves as grasshoppers. They had a slave mentality leftover from Egypt and even God's powerful signs, wonders and provisions weren't enough for them to trust Him. Their grasshopper mentality resulted in their refusal to go to war and take the land. With the exception of Joshua and Caleb, who believed the Lord could defeat the giants, the rest perished in the wilderness, even though the Lord's plan had always been to bring them in.

Many times we base our confidence and faith on outward circumstances instead of on what God has told us He will do. *We have to anchor our faith in who He is, rather than in what we can do in our own strength.*

So what or who are the giants in your land? What are the strongholds that rob you of faith and enslave you to fear? We need to cry out for a fresh revelation of God's awesomeness. As you believe God and even take baby steps in faith, He will give you the key strategies to do the impossible. God never saw His people as grasshoppers. Rather, *He saw the giants as grasshoppers!*

God wants you to have faith to believe His promises and His unshakable abilities. The key to conquering new territory in the Spirit and taking out giants is to take the first step—to trust and believe that He is able to do it! Take that leap of faith and be a radical Joshua who will take out the giants in your land.

Prayer: *Lord, forgive me for taking my eyes off of You and looking at the giants. Help me to not have a grasshopper mentality, not moving in fear but in faith. Forgive me for my unbelief. Even as the Israelites needed to go to war and trust You for the strategies, I also want to be courageous and trust You for the victories on my homefront. I want to radically seize the territory that You have entrusted to me!*

Day 8 – Joshua's Journey: The Key to the Secret Place

Exodus 33:11

The Lord spoke to Moses face to face, as a man speaks to his friend. And he would return to the camp, but his servant Joshua, the son of Nun, did not depart from the tabernacle.

Joshua became Moses' successor. He was in charge of taking the Children of Israel into the Promised Land. How was he prepared by the Lord for this mammoth task? He spent forty years in the secret place—*while in the wilderness!* When Moses met the Lord in the Tent of Meeting, Joshua would stay around the tent and linger in the Presence. Exodus 33:11b says, "Moses' young aide, Joshua... did not leave the tent." Numbers 27:18 refers to Joshua as one in whom the Spirit dwelt.

The Lord made a covenant with Joshua and told him, "Everywhere you put the sole of your foot, I will give it to you. Be strong and of good courage and do not be afraid, for I am with you all the days of your life. I am going to give you possession of the land (Joshua 1:3-4)." Then the Lord gave Joshua several instructions, among which was the challenge to, "determine to earnestly seek God's presence throughout your life."

God whispered divine war strategies to His intimate friend! Joshua had to hear the Lord's voice to survive as God's next appointed leader and he did not underestimate the power of his prayers. Many of us look at prayer as a one-way conversation. But beloved, prayer is a dialogue in which God wants to download strategic war plans, blueprints from Heaven and keys to, "open doors that no man can shut and shut doors that no man can open (Isaiah 22:22)." There is power in your prayers.

The hotter the battle, the greater the need to stop, wait and receive instructions. God wants soldiers whose every move will be an obedient act to their Commander in Chief. As Oswald Chambers wrote, "Prayer does not fit us for the greater works; prayer *is* the greater work."

Prayer: *Oh Lord, I know that You are calling me into the secret place. Teach me the power of prayer! Release a spirit of prayer and intercession so that I can go to the war rooms in Heaven, get divine blueprints and then win earthly battles. Teach me how to war in the heavenlies before we even battle here on Earth.*

Day 9 – Joshua's Journey:
Rahab and the Two Spies

Hebrews 11:30-31

By faith the walls of Jericho fell, after the people had marched around them for seven days. By faith the prostitute, Rahab, because she welcomed the spies, was not killed with those who were disobedient.

Matthew 1:5-6

Salmon begot boaz by Rahab... and Jesse begot David, the King.

Joshua sent two spies into Jericho. As they were hunted, they desperately sought refuge. Where did they find a safe haven? In a religious temple? No. Hiding for their very lives, their refuge was found in the most unlikely place! The door that they entered was open for many—a prostitute's house of trade. Rahab, a Canaanite, was an enemy to the Law of Moses as well as a woman of ill repute. *It is so important to realize how significant this is.* In Jericho, their sanctuary and safety was found in the den of the enemy—a pagan prostitute's house!

As God starts to take you into the Jerichos of your life, He asks if you are willing to knock on unlikely and unreligious doors. Hearing God's voice was not an option for the spies, but a survival mechanism, as they would be executed if they were caught. If they had not learned the Lord's voice in the wilderness, they would not have been prepared for the invasion of Jericho that awaited them. Are you willing to press in to hear the Lord's voice and move in radical and non-religious strategies? God does not want you to rely on human reasoning or on religious law, but to lean into Him for fresh blueprint plans (Pr. 3:5-6). This can save your life in a critical moment, even as the spies were spared.

Rahab hid the Israelite spies, even at the expense of her own family, and in return, all she asked was that her family be spared. She was like an early Corrie Ten Boom who hid the Jews in WWII. What is so remarkable about this woman of trade is that after the invasion of Jericho, she married a captain in Joshua's army. Joshua's battle did much more than just tear down the walls of Jericho—he rescued a bride. For out of her seed came King David, and later Jesus. What if they had never knocked on her door?

Rahab is a prophetic picture of the end-time Church. The Bride of Christ will be birthed from the most unlikely of places. God's love will transform a whore into a heroine, a harlot into a pure and spotless Bride. The Lord wants to take off our blinders. Are you willing to find the Rahabs? What is the 21st century translation of a modern-day Rahab? She may wear designer clothes and frequent the mall, but she is desperately looking for love in all the wrong places. The Lord wants us to take off our religious blinders and partner with Him to find His Bride.

Prayer: Oh Lord, I must know and feel Your heart for Your people. I don't want to religiously write off the Rahabs—I want to rescue them. Help me to look past the sin and love the sinner. Help me to go to the unlikely, overlooked, unlovely places, bringing salvation and healing to Your wounded Bride.

Day 10 – Joshua's Journey: Radical Visitation for Divine Strategies

Hebrews 11:30

By faith the walls of Jericho fell, after the people had marched around them for seven days.

Another strategy Joshua received was a radical visitation from the Captain of the Host. He said to Joshua, "See, I have delivered Jericho into your hands, along with its king and fighting men." Then He gave Joshua divine strategies on how to take down Jericho. Joshua's first response to this unusual battle plan must have been, "Huh? Did you say *trumpets*? Don't you mean spears, knives, arrows, shields and battering rams?"

Picture this: their fearless leader has returned with a heavenly battle strategy that will bring sure victory and take them into the Promised Land. The anticipation reaches a fevered pitch and Joshua says, "Good news, men, the Captain of the Hosts appeared to me." The men whoop and yell, jabbing the air with their swords and waving their shields. "The bad news is, He gave me the battle plan." Kicking the sand with his toe, Joshua mumbles to the confused soldiers, "Uh... marching... priests... trumpets... ark... shouting... and the walls should fall down."

We've pretty much become immune to the story of Jericho because it's so well known, but let's stop and really see it again with fresh eyes. What an incredible story! What a unique strategy! No commander on earth would plan for battle like that. What great faith he had to go to war when his front line of protection was a group of trumpet-playing priests. But you know the song's happy ending, "... and the walls came a'tumblin' down."

In times of great weakness, when Joshua could only depend on the Lord, the strategies he received were truly unusual and creative. The Lord required prophetic acts that would seem utterly ridiculous to the natural mind. Marching seven times around the city while blowing a horn and believing that the walls would fall? Preposterous! Hiding in a brothel? Scandalous!

Our God is incredible and creative, moving with supernatural miracle power in the midst of our trust and obedience to Him, even in the midst of what seems simple or ridiculous. But the Lord knew the exact timing and strategy to take down that fortified city.

Prayer: Lord, we want the walls to tumble down around our city! Help us to do radical exploits for You—using trumpets as weapons and worship as warfare! Help us to take new territory in the Spirit for You!

Day 11 – Do You Want a Visitation?

Genesis 28:12

Then he [Jacob] dreamed, and behold, a ladder was set up on the Earth, and its top reached to Heaven; and there the angels of God were ascending and descending...

I want to impart to you a holy jealousy to have a life-changing visitation with Jesus.

I was ministering in New Zealand in 1992 at a meeting where God literally showed up! I was staying with a pastor and his wife in Christchurch, New Zealand, that had a church of about 150 people in the inner-city. The people were poor but they had a desperate hunger for the Lord. The Sunday morning meeting had a low spiritual ceiling, so after lunch I desperately asked the Lord for a breakthrough that night. I saw an open vision of a holy tornado over the city and I saw myself as a tiny spark of fire going into this whirlwind of glory. I didn't know what it meant.

That night during worship, the atmosphere began to change—it became saturated with the tangible glory of the Lord! In fact, many of us could hear the voices of angels singing with the worship. I felt that Heaven was invading Earth.

The crowd had just taken their seats. As I was about to begin, I felt the Lord behind me and when I looked, I saw a huge tidal wave of glory as tall as the ceiling coming into the meeting. I asked, "Wow, Lord! What are we supposed to do with this?"

He told me to have the people stand up. I obeyed and told them what I saw. As the first tidal wave started to roll into the room, the Lord said, "This one is for impartation." As the wave came in, the people were radically gripped by the Lord. Scores of people went down sovereignly all over the room, their hearts tenderized and empowered as His glory washed over them. Laughter and weeping erupted throughout the room.

Then I looked behind me and once again another tidal wave of glory was beginning to crest. The Lord said, "This one is for deliverance. Tell them to get up again." Quickly the people responded as another wave crashed over them. People screamed, slithered on the floor like snakes, and were radically delivered from demonic oppression.

A third wave began to roll through the room, the Lord said, "This one is for physical healing." Once again the people got up and were healed. Seven waves of glory moved through the room that night and left them radically undone. This took about an hour, so I asked the Lord what I should preach about. He said, "I want you to share on having a childlike heart." After about 15 minutes of preaching, the heavens opened up and I saw a Jacob's ladder come into the middle of the room, with angels ascending and descending. They were carrying mantles and hot coals of fire. The room became alive with His manifest presence. Several dozen people began to dance with angels. Impartation and the joy of the Lord also came. Hours later the *kabod*, the weighty glory of the Lord, was very tangible as the Lord continued to heal bodies, minds and spirits.

Truly, Heaven had come down and kissed Earth. No one was left untouched! Revival broke out in the city for several years as huge crowds hungered for God. Do you want a visitation?

———

Prayer: Lord, I must have a visitation! Release the fiery whirlwind of Your presence with fresh anointing and impartation of Your heart into my heart. I want an open heaven over my life. I'm desperate for a profound touch from You, Lord!

Day 12 – Prophetic Intercession for the Nations

Jeremiah 23:21-22

I have not sent these prophets, yet they ran. I have not spoken to them, yet they prophesied. But if they had stood in My counsel, and had caused My people to hear My words, then they would have turned them from their evil way and from the evil of their doings.

Rees Howells was a radical intercessor during World War II whose prophetic revelation changed the course of the nations. Seeing in the heavens and knowing the plans of the enemy, he was able to then sabotage those schemes before they were fulfilled and release the plans of the Lord.

I want to share a testimony about the power of prophetic intercession. This *kairos* hour in history demands that we must know the times and seasons. Can we go into the counsel of the Lord and get the fresh strategies and war plans for today?

During the Gulf War, I kept seeing the same battles taking place on television. I started to get very frustrated and said, "Lord, I don't want just natural television. I want Your 'tell-a-vision.' I want to see what is happening in the heavens over the Middle East. Lord, what is on Your heart? There must be more information. I feel the American government is showing us bits and pieces, but Lord, what are You doing in the realm of the Spirit?"

On Sunday morning my pastor of a congregation of 3,000 told us to stand and pray for Israel. All of a sudden I heard the audible voice of the Lord saying, "Michael." I asked, "Michael who?" He said, "Michael, the Archangel." Suddenly I had an open vision of Michael fighting over Israel. I asked the Lord what He was doing. Instantly I saw the Prince of Persia and Michael in a fierce battle. The Lord continued, "The Prince of Persia is trying to preempt My timetable so that's why I've released Michael. The war will end in three days."

The Lord spoke again and He said, "Gabriel." I asked, "Lord, what is he doing?" Immediately I saw Gabriel moving families and individuals so they wouldn't be harmed. The next night I was at a Baptist pastor's house and met a pastor from Israel. As I shook his hand I said, "I saw Michael over Israel. The war is going to end on the third day." He said, "Michael is the archangel over Israel." When the pastor was flying back to Israel on Purim, the war ended that very day, which was three days later.

You see, you must be willing to have your antennas up twenty-four hours a day, seven days a week. Ask the Lord strategic questions about your life, family, work, school, city and world events. The Lord is raising up prophets in this hour who will go into the counsels of the Lord. Intercession, fasting and worship accelerate the call of God on each of our lives. Are you available to go deeper into the war room of God?

Prayer: Lord, I'm so spiritually blind. Open my eyes so that I can see what is happening in the realm of the Spirit. I so want to pray dangerous prayers that can stop the plans of the enemy and release Your power. I want to hear Your voice and know Your ways. Help me to pray in a way that establishes Heaven on Earth so that Your will is done.

Day 13 – Hearing the Voice of God

Hosea 4:6

My people are destroyed for lack of knowledge.

Beloved, hearing the Lord's voice is not an option. It is survival! We are all called to the prophetic lifestyle and to be naturally supernatural. Prophecy is not just reserved for an elite platform ministry. The Lord wants us to hear His voice in everyday life and know how to pray for our loved ones.

However, we must remember that learning how to hear the voice of the Lord is a process. Sometimes you will just get an impression, a prompting, a feeling, a picture or a knowing. Here's the key: God wants us to love Him so much so that we are willing to risk, to be foolish and to step out with those impressions. If we are faithful in the little, He will give us more. Do you have your antennas up in the Holy Spirit? Waiting for the next prophet to roll into town, just to get a word and transcribe it in your archives?

There must be tenacity in you where you wrestle with God to hear His voice. The Lord asks us to come to Him as little children. Often He will only give me part of the word. As I step out, I then get the next part of it. Don't wait for a full technicolor vision projected on the wall before you start talking! Start with the small impressions and more will follow. I realize that it is scary to walk on water, but honestly, beloved, it is more frightening to stay in the boat.

It's time to seize our inheritance as a prophetic people. Hearing from God is your birthright. Ask the Holy Spirit to teach you. People's very lives depend on our willingness to hear the voice of God. Be a divine detective and ask the Lord to take you through the School of the Holy Spirit. *Willingness will take us further in the Kingdom of God than perfection.*

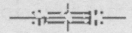

Prayer: *Oh Lord, help me to grow up in You. I want to hear Your voice and I want You to use my life to bring others to You! Teach me to take my prayers as seriously as You do and help me to remember that the power of life and death is in my tongue. Lord, teach me how to pray.*

Day 14 – Revival Starts with You

2 Chronicles 16:9

For the eyes of the Lord range throughout the Earth to strengthen those whose hearts are fully committed to Him.

I believe that revival is not born out of mass movements but out of a series of solitary decisions.

Over the last several years, I have traveled to more churches and nations than I can count. Many have gathered together and called others to pray, to fast and to walk in unity. At first the meetings are packed by the mounting momentum of trying out the latest, greatest new idea. Then, slowly, the meetings dwindle down; one or two intercessors are the sole watchmen left on the wall. The faithful few glumly look around at the empty rows of chairs.

We get discouraged when we don't see others manifesting the same enthusiasm for revival that we have. We worry, "How can our city be transformed unless the pastor of that major church is involved and all the meetings are filled?" But I tell you, beloved, God is not focused on the empty chairs. Rather, He is focused on the chairs that are filled.

You are there.

And He has drawn you there. He is going to begin His work with you. Revival starts today. Revival starts with you. He has hand-chosen you, before the foundations of the world, to embark on a journey into the fullness of your destiny. Do you want to be His voice rather than just another man's echo?

If so, will you return to Him as your first love? Remember, God must first set our hearts ablaze with radical passion for Jesus. Intimacy is what ignites revolution.

Is the presence of the living God fully taking up residence in your heart? If that has not happened, then why are you expecting that to happen in some kind of public meeting? Revival starts with *you!* Personal transformation must precede city transformation. Let a revolution begin today—and may it begin within you!

Prayer: Oh Lord, I ask that You would radically revolutionize my life from the inside out. Cause revival to burn so deeply in my heart that others can't help but be changed. Oh Lord, You are truly all I want! Tenderize my heart again so I desire to return to You as my first love. Where my heart has drifted and gotten lukewarm, return me back to You. God, I give You permission to do whatever it takes to make me wholly Yours. Set my heart on fire! Set my spirit ablaze today!

Day 15 – The Power of Prayer

Jeremiah 33:3

Call unto Me and I will answer you and show you great and mighty things.

Sincere and passionate prayer is the key to unlock our relationship with Almighty God. Many struggle with praying because they feel that their intercession is not much more than empty cries to an invisible God who seems so distant. We think that our prayers shoot only as high as the ceiling and then bounce back unheard and unanswered. But beloved, God loves communing with you. He promises that He will hear us and answer.

In fact, *communing with God is the highest purpose for which you were created!* "This is eternal life: to know Me (John 17)." Our hunger for God Himself is what fuels our prayer life. When His presence is our passion and our hunger is for His heart, we can approach the throne of God boldly with the confidence that our Daddy loves our prayers, but having this first love is so important. As John Bunyan said, "In prayer it is better to have a heart without words than words without a heart."

A key to prayer is listening. Remember, God has more to say to you than you have to say to Him. James 4:8 promises, "Draw nigh unto God and He will draw nigh unto you." Drawing near to Him, free from distractions, with a heart to first worship and commune with Him is where we must begin. He holds the answers to all your questions before they are even on your lips. Listen for His voice.

Another key in unlocking the resources of Heaven with our intercession is to pray with the Bible. Like Jacob did in Genesis 32, we can remind God about what He said. God's Word does not return to Him void, and if we remind God of

His promises, we can have confidence that whatever we ask, according to His will, is heard and answered.

A final point of caution is that the ultimate goal in prayer is not to have our prayers answered, but to encounter God Himself. Fellowship and intimacy are not based upon the hours you spend in prayer. Rather, intimacy is the time you spend with God. Prayer cannot just be storming the gates of Heaven with a list of requests as an empty exercise of words. Rather, our prayers must be desperate cries for encounter from our heart to His heart! Having the audience of God is not something to take lightly. It is an incredible honor to rest in the knowledge that the omniscient, ever-powerful God of the universe has one joy above all else—and that is to spend time with *you*!

***

Prayer: Oh Lord, I want to have a passion for Your presence. Dig deep into my inner soul and help me to not fear the setting apart with You. Oh, how I ache to know You more! Teach me to pray the prayers that stir Your heart. I want to minister to You with my prayers. I want my heart to bless Your heart and to give You the love that You deserve!

Day 16 – Fresh Revelation
Face-to-Face

Exodus 33:15-16

Then Moses said to [the Lord], "If Your presence does not go with us, do not send us up from here. How will anyone know that You are pleased with me and with Your people unless You go with us? What else will distinguish me and Your people from all the other people on the face of the Earth?"

After an incredible "mountaintop" experience on Mount Sinai with a 40-day visitation, receiving the Ten Commandments and having God inscribe the Law on his heart, Moses descended the mountain and was hit with heavy spiritual warfare. His people were entangled in blatant sexual perversion as they worshipped a golden calf. The Lord's jealousy burned and He released judgment, costing three thousand men their lives.

In total desperation, Moses cried out for a greater encounter with the Lord—a deeper visitation was needed! It was not enough to see a burning bush, or watch the Red Sea part, or even see supernatural provision each day with the raining down of manna. He cried out for more. He wanted to see God's face. He would not take "No" for an answer. Total desperation, unquenchable hunger and unswerving commitment to his people caused Moses to contend with God for His presence.

While Moses faced death and warfare, it caused him to press into God with a greater desperation. Do your trials cause you to run *to* God or *from* God? No matter what your circumstances, God is inviting you to come up higher. Don't live in the valley of death and destroyed dreams. He will give you the strength and the wings of an eagle to soar up the mountain to greater heights in Him.

God answered Moses' cry by letting His goodness pass before him. After Moses descended, the very glory of God rested on him, causing his face to shine. Moses even had to wear a veil to hide the blinding brightness of God's glory.

Have you, like Moses, cried out to see the face of God? It is not enough to have a mountaintop experience or receive fresh revelation as Moses did. Moses wanted more.

He wanted friendship. He wanted intimacy. He wanted God Himself. There is something greater than receiving life-changing prophetic words, attending the latest of conferences or seeing God's power explode in signs and wonders.

Nothing is greater in this life than being His friend. Is there a cry in you for a deeper friendship with God? God is calling for us to meet with Him face-to-face.

Prayer: Lord, the warfare has been so intense. In the storms of life, I want to run to You and not from You. What I have had before is just not enough. I need to see You face to face. I want to be Your friend and hear Your heart. Please encounter me, Lord!

Day 17 – Running to Him, Not From Him: Godly Fear

Exodus 14:31

And when the Israelites saw the great power the Lord displayed against the Egyptians, the people feared the Lord and put their trust in Him and in Moses, His servant.

Fear, or reverential awe of the Lord, should help us run *to* God rather than *from* God. Moses' encounter with God on Mount Sinai is an awesome example of how encountering God causes reverence and elation, rather than fear of rejection and spiritual boredom.

Moses ascended the great mountain of the Lord, shielded from the glare of life's non-essentials. This was the place where God is all that exists and all that matters. After the lightning and the rumblings on Mount Sinai, Moses returned and told the people something interesting. He said, "God has come to place His fear in you so that you might not sin."

Godly fear is a reverential awe. It is realized with an encounter with another-world, extra-dimensional, supernatural reality. And in that place of realization, it empowers our hearts to not settle for the lesser loves of this world.

We find casual, routine religion to be convenient. We find it to be pleasant. But this kind of religion fails to provide the average American parishioner, week in and week out, with the kind of spine-tingling, edge-of-the-seat environment that delivers us from lesser distractions. Personally, I am easily bored when I can predict every moment of a church service. God is radical and unpredictable; He wants to fascinate me and I want to be fascinated by Him. He wants to bring in the "suddenly" of His personality.

When Moses went up onto Mount Sinai, he didn't think that he was going to have forty minutes of worship, then some announcements, and then the timed message. When God is in the house, nothing is predictable! If His presence is there, you are on the edge of your seat and you forget your watch; you don't know how much time has passed. God is there and that is all that matters. Do not let your hearts faint if there is a holy dissatisfaction burning in you. For the most radical encounters that you will have will be in the privacy of your own home in the secret place. You must contend for that something more and let that hunger drive you into a deeper intimacy with Him. Let's all cry out for our own Mount Sinai encounters with the Lord.

We must have more of You, Father!

***

Prayer: *Lord, I want to have a holy fear of Your awesomeness. Help me to climb the mountain, to encounter You and to not settle for anything less than You alone. We welcome You back to our churches to ruin us for the ordinary. We must have Your presence or we will become dull and barren!*

Day 18 – Behind the Veil: Heaven Touching Earth in Worship

Revelation 4:1

After this I looked, and there before me was a door standing open in Heaven. And the voice I had first heard speaking to me like a trumpet said, "Come up here, and I will show you what must take place after this."

My goal in worship is to get behind the veil. My passion is His presence. His presence is manna that must be sought after and received every single day or it becomes stale. There is one thing that God cannot deny—humans hungering for Him.

How hungry are you? Are you willing to passionately press through into His presence? Beloved, He must first deal with your heart. One key to unlock worship is first asking the Lord if there is anything hindering us in our heart. As I work through stripping off all sin and self before the Lord, it is as though I trade in my rags for His robes of righteousness. Then, He can begin to give you His heart, His purposes, His love for you and His people.

During worship there is so much activity happening in the supernatural. It is when the creative presence of the Lord God touches His people. Some people see pictures, hear scriptures, get a word of knowledge, or hear His voice. All of it is valid, real and scriptural. But what does worship really do?

Worship moves the very heart of God and changes the very heart of man. It takes only a few seconds of a face-to-face encounter with the manifest presence of God to change the course of human history for you, your city, or your nation.

In the Old Testament, His presence was often referred to as the shekinah glory, the fire of divine visitation. God would literally come to visit His people. In 2 Chronicles 5:14 the glory of God filled Solomon's Temple and the priests could not stand to minister. The thick weight of the presence of God settled in so heavily that people would have to lay flat on the floor, prostrate before Him. Never underestimate the power of worship.

"What can make the angels cry? Cause their wings to hide their eyes?"[1] His beauty can! Worship is encountering Him. It is an invitation to the place where angels cannot go, beyond the very boundary lines in Heaven where God will whisper to you the secrets of His burning heart. You will hear the love songs of God's heart and return them back as songs to Him.

Prayer: Lord, awaken my heart to worship You. I want to be one who desires You alone rather than just what You can give me or how You can use me. I want to be able to see what the angels see, go into Your throne room, encounter Your beauty and be ravished by Your love. When songs become familiar and routine, burn a fresh fire in my heart so that worship will transport me into Your very heart.

---

[1] Note: Lyric excerpt from JoAnn McFatter's "Raging Beauty" CD www.joannmcfatter.com

Day 19 – The Least Shall Be the Greatest: Humility

James 4:6, 7, 10

But He gives more grace. Therefore He says, "God resists the proud, but gives grace to the humble." Therefore submit to God. Resist the devil and he will flee from you... Humble yourselves in the sight of the Lord, and He will lift you up.

Years ago when ministering in the nation of New Zealand, I was given an open-eyed vision that changed my life. I saw an enormous fiery angel full of the glory of the Lord walking up and down the nation. He was brandishing a mighty sword that was beheading those who were standing tall in their own pride, egotism and self-glory. The Lord was dealing with the haughty attitude of their hearts through this powerful angel.

Those who were bowed low on their faces, postured in humility, were spared, knighted and promoted. The Lord was raising them up to a new place of leadership because of their meekness and humility of heart.

God requires and honors humility. If you want your life to have significance, then position yourself at the feet of Jesus.

As I have ministered in numerous conferences, I've seen many people moving in self-promotion and climbing the corporate ladder of ministry through church politics. Honestly, this breaks the very heart of God. It also tests our hearts when we are overlooked and others are unfairly promoted above us. The Lord allows these fires to work a death in our own hearts, killing our pride and desire for position.

We cannot use people—prostituting His bride—to build our name, ministry or personal mailing lists. The goal is to be so accepted and confident in His love that we do not need the limelight because we are so in love with the Light of the World, the glorious Man, Christ Jesus.

At the end of the day, His opinion is the only one that counts. When we are so rooted and grounded in His affections, it is easy to not care about promoting ourselves. It is then that we find ourselves in that wonderful place of reckless abandonment—of being a laid-down lover of Jesus—and our lives are truly all about Him.

There is a price behind the anointing. The years of being overlooked are a fiery inferno, but the Lord can use it to work gold in our hearts. The challenge in this life-long journey is to keep our hearts soft, humble and bowed low before Him. Our gifts will make room for us in due season. Do we have love and humility regardless of what happened to us, or have we become disqualified because of bitterness and hardness of heart?

Prayer: Lord, help me to stay on the operating table as You perform heart surgery. Make me so rooted and grounded in Your love that I don't promote myself. Give me grace and humility to accept Your timing and orchestration of my life.

Day 20 – Bridal Garments of Humility

Isaiah 62:4-5

You shall no longer be termed Forsaken, nor shall your land any more be termed Desolate; but you shall be called Hephzibah, and your land Beulah; for the Lord delights in you, and your land shall be married... and as the Bridegroom rejoices over the Bride, so shall your God rejoice over you.

One of the greatest, most breathtaking moments in a wedding is watching the bride promenade down the aisle, wrapped in the most glorious of garments. The crowd is hushed and all eyes are affixed for she has captured the room just by her appearance.

Even today, Holy Spirit is training us in humility to rule and reign with Him as His Bride. If the Bride is to be equally yoked to the Bridegroom, she must wear the same wedding garments He wore. If Jesus, the King of Kings, chose a crown of thorns, how much more should we adorn ourselves in the beauty of meekness? If He forsook His divine robes of righteousness for earthly burlap robes, how much more should we wrap ourselves in a mantle of humility?

At the Marriage Supper of the Lamb, each one of us will be wrapped in different garments, brilliantly embroidered with the fruits and rewards from our earthly lives. A stunning, colorful, tailor-made royal robe will be our portion.

In the Lord's great wisdom, it's as though the outer garment that covered each person was a simple burlap robe—a mantle of humility. Underneath that robe is the beautiful royal robe of our giftings. The Lord displays these at different times, but most of the time it is a secret testimony between you and the Lord.

Walking in humility is a heart issue, a lifestyle, an attitude that is God-given. *An impartation of humility is different than a decision of humility.* You can't instantaneously grow humility in your heart. Rather, it is a journey of a lifetime of matching your heart with God's heart. Ask God to do whatever it takes to make you a pure reflection of His Son.

Prayer: Lord, I give You permission to do whatever it takes to kill my pride. Help me to be the first one to run to the cross, humble myself and say yes to You, Lord—always. I need Your help to forgive and always put other people before me, just as You sacrificed everything for me. I want to cloak myself in a garment of humility so I am a Bride who matches her Husband.

Day 21 – When You Dance With God, Let Him Lead

1 Corinthians 1:2

But God has chosen the foolish things of the world to put to shame the wise, and God has chosen the weak things of the world to put to shame the things which are mighty.

God does not like to be put under a microscope. Perfectionism, performance-driven and program-oriented attitudes will hinder us from moving in the Holy Spirit.

He is asking all of us to be flexible and to let Him be God. We offend Him by the little boxes we put Him in and by the different ways religion tries to control Him. We say, "everything should be done in decency and order," but beloved, there is something greater than our logical human order: *He has a divine order.* Divine order was for His Son, Jesus, to spit on the ground, make clay with His saliva, and spread it on a man's eyes so that he would be healed. That doesn't sound too orderly. Are you willing to move in His divine order and not be so logical and fenced in by formulas that you miss the move of Holy Spirit altogether?

Guess what? God is God, and we are not! So, let Him be God. Often God will move in ways that offend your mind because He wants to test your heart. I feel like the Lord is asking us, "Are you really willing to follow Me, even if you don't always understand my rhyme and reason? Are you really willing to make mistakes and be in the School of the Holy Spirit?"

Most of us are more concerned about protecting our own reputations than really being consumed with the fame of His name. Are we willing to step out of the boat in faith, even if we are sometimes wrong or get rejected? *What are you willing to risk to learn to hear the Lord?* We need to be willing to do anything for God—even make mistakes.

We must make a covenant to be available to however God wants to use us. In my journey of being a weak and broken vessel, I purposed in my heart not to just fall back on the four spiritual laws, or other religious tools that we can pull out of our bag of ministry tricks. But rather, I want to be willing to be a fool for Jesus. In the midst of not always knowing why God tells us to do something, we must do what He says simply because we love Him. Do not be afraid to jump off cliffs for God. Another way to spell faith is R-I-S-K!

—:⁞≡⁞≡⁞:—

Prayer: *Lord, forgive me for putting You in a box. Let Your fire come and baptize me with Your Holy Spirit. Burn up all the religion and control. Teach me how to minister to those whose hearts are broken or need physical or emotional healing. Teach me to let You lead and to simply follow You!*

Day 22 – Mary's Prophetic Journey

Luke 1:38

Then Mary said, "Behold the maidservant of the Lord! Let it be to me according to your word." And the angel departed from her.

Our prophetic history with God is a never-ending cyclical journey. We each have seasons with prophetic revelation, spiritual warfare leading to the wilderness, the ho-hum of ordinary life and times of ministry which take us to the cross. These sequences leading to periods of resurrection make us carriers of the glory as we pass through persecution and the fires of life. Then, the never-ending cycle begins again with seasons of renewal and visitations.

One incredible biblical example of this is Mary, the mother of Jesus. So often we think of her as a 15-year old riding away on a donkey to facilitate the Christmas story, but let's look at the tapestry of her *whole* life. Just like us, she was on a prophetic journey, cloaked in mysteries that unraveled gradually.

Mary's radical visitation with Gabriel's stunning announcement—Elizabeth's Magnificat—involved angelic choirs serenading country shepherds, the Magi's trek from the East bringing gifts, Anna and Simeon's testimony at the temple, radical impartation and constant divine orchestrations. It all died with His shattered body at Golgotha, only to be resurrected. So let's begin this wonderful journey.

A radical visitation came one night when the angel Gabriel came to Mary. "Me, can you imagine," Mary thought! She was young and simple... a Jewish girl living in poverty in the little town of Nazareth. What did she have to offer anyone, especially Almighty God?

Gabriel's voice filled her whole room and she was terrified. "Greetings, you who are highly favored among women. The Lord is with you." He told her not to fear and that she would give birth to the Messiah. Mary cried out, "Yes, Lord let it be unto me according to Your word."

The Holy Spirit overshadowed Mary. A radical impartation of the fiery seed of the Father pierced her womb and impregnated her with Jesus. This ushered in the Messianic Age and it was the fulfillment of all the Old Testament prophecies and the Law.

Mary possessed a heart of devotion and childlike faith. She was a sovereign vessel chosen to be the mother of Jesus, yet the Bible never indicates that she moved in miracles. She simply said, "Yes, Lord, let it be done unto me, according to Your word," and it changed her life forever. *That's why we can all be like Mary.* Her life was a tapestry of prayer, purity and humility.

Do you want a visitation? Cry out, "Lord, I want to be like Mary! I want to be radically overshadowed by the Holy Spirit to bring revival. Lord, I want to be your intercessor, impregnated with your purposes!"

There is a price behind the anointing. There is a stigma. Birthing the things of the Spirit is always messy and revival is always controversial. Are you willing to be a manger and birth Jesus, or are you one who says, "There's no room in the inn?"

Prayer: Lord, like Mary, I want to be radically overshadowed by Your Spirit and impregnated with Your purposes. No matter what the cost, no matter what others think, I say to You, "Let it be done unto me!"

Day 23 – Mary's Prophetic Journey: Heavy Spiritual Warfare

Matthew 2:16

Then Herod, when he saw that he was deceived by the wise men, was exceedingly angry; and he sent forth and put to death all the male children who were in Bethlehem and in all its districts, from two years old and under.

"In the middle of the night Joseph shook me violently. He was terrified, crying, ranting about Herod wanting Jesus dead and something about leaving town—now. He grabbed Jesus and was out the door before I could even understand. We left everything behind that night, no explanations, no good-byes. Fifteen minutes and life as we knew it was over. I looked back one last time as I left my hometown. I didn't know we would be in hiding for years," Mary thought.

Why did King Herod feel so threatened by an unassuming little baby wrapped in swaddling clothes tucked in a manger in Bethlehem? We must realize that this is much more than merely Herod persecuting the Jews in the natural. Rather, when Jesus was born, the Kingdom of God invaded Earth. Therefore, this was a confrontation with a supernatural clashing of two governmental powers. The Kingdom of God broke forth on Earth, and Satan knew it. So, in rage, the demonic realm retaliated in order to kill Jesus before He could fulfill the will of the Father. Suddenly, when the appointed time came, Satan responded with vengeance.

Satan goes after the move of God in its infancy, when it is most vulnerable. Jesus' birth necessitated an escape from Herod's slaughtering army. They were given divine strategies and were hidden in the enemy's camp—Egypt.

When you have had radical encounters, profound prophetic words and visitations from the Lord, the enemy then wants to snatch the seeds of your destiny before this word can be planted and established. The greater your call and destiny is, the greater the spiritual warfare.

So expect an onslaught of attack because the enemy wants to abort your prophetic promises. But when Jesus moves radically in your life, it will birth revival and renewal. This, in turn, always brings shaking in every arena of your life—relationships, jobs, ministries and anything that is dear to your heart. When the stirrings of revival are being birthed, it rouses the demonic realm to challenge the status quo. Often those closest to us will be the first to cast stones, and the enemy uses unexpected people to shoot arrows of discouragement into our hearts.

But be encouraged beloved, the enemy doesn't waste his time. If you don't make Satan nervous by your radical abandonment to Jesus, perhaps you should re-evaluate your choices. So if you are in a heavy battle, be encouraged. The enemy must really consider you a threat!

Prayer: *Lord, give me wisdom and strategies to escape the Herods of my life and wait upon the fulfillment of the prophetic promises of my life. Help me to follow Your lead, and teach me to only fight the battles You have called me to. I am willing to find refuge, even in the wilderness. Help me to know when to withdraw and when to fight. I want to be so hidden in You that I am invisible to the enemy.*

Day 24 – Mary's Prophetic Journey: The Wilderness

Hosea 2:14

Therefore I am now going to allure her; I will lead her into the wilderness and speak tenderly to her.

Luke 2:19

But Mary treasured up all these things and pondered them in her heart.

"Why Egypt? Why pagan Egypt? It's the land of bondage for our people," Mary ponders. "Moses led us out. Will we die there like our forefathers? We live as refugees. I keep wondering why God didn't just remove Herod. Why did we have to flee into the night? Those back home must be grieving terribly. They don't even know where we are or what happened to us. I wish they could see Jesus grow up. I wish He could scamper onto His grandmother's lap and she could wrap her arms around Him and rock Him to sleep. He was her delight."

You've had incredible dramatic encounters with God and you've had multiple prophetic words on tape and transcribed them into notebooks. You're sure that any minute your prophetic promises will happen. Remember the words that someday you'd have a platform ministry and move in miraculous healing?

Mary also received prophetic words: Her Son would be the King of the Jews. So why were they banished and suffering in an uncomfortable and foreign land? Mary didn't realize that the prophetic timetable for the fulfillment of Jesus' destiny would be a grueling thirty years! You, too, will spend time in the wilderness seasons of barrenness. Are you willing to wait on the Lord's timing?

"Finally, after several years in Egypt, God spoke to Joseph again in a dream. Herod was dead. This time it was I (Mary) who grabbed Jesus and ran out the door with Joseph trailing behind. We couldn't get home fast enough!"

Do you feel as if you're on a shelf, living an ordinary life? Are you changing diapers, cooking dinner and dealing with the neighbors while crying out in your heart, "Lord, have you forgotten me? Why don't people recognize my gifting? Don't they realize I had a radical visitation back in 1998?"

Mary had thirty years of obscurity to develop a hidden testimony—a secret history with God. You, too, have an appointed time to build family, community and greater intimacy with Jesus. In the midst of that time you may feel like crying out, "What's taking so long? By the time my destiny comes, I'll be pursuing it in a wheelchair!" But seasons of preparation are important. These are the times when God works patience, radical passion and deep devotion into your life.

Prayer: Lord, draw me away and speak tenderly to my heart. Teach me to embrace the wilderness seasons of my life. Help me to make You the final goal rather than ministry. Teach me to encounter You even in the midst of everyday life. I want to develop a secret history with You, Lord. I love You so very much!

Day 25 – Mary's Prophetic Journey: Finally, Ministry Begins!

Matthew 12:48

But He answered and said to the one who told Him, "Who is My mother and who are My brothers?" And He stretched out His hand toward His disciples and said, "Here are My mother and My brothers! For whoever does the will of My Father in Heaven is My brother and sister and mother."

After a radical visitation, the birth of Jesus, escaping to Egypt as a refugee, coming back to Nazareth and living an ordinary life for thirty years, finally His ministry begins! A great revival of signs and wonders sweeps the land.

"When I was forty-five years old, life changed dramatically, for Jesus and me (Mary). He started bringing home a ragtag bunch of fishermen to dinner. He never could resist a stray. Then we were at a wedding and He changed water to wine. Now He's moving in signs and wonders. In the blink of an eye He has a huge crowd following Him everywhere. It's been a long time coming, but I can see now that with this popularity, He will soon be King of the Jews."

"Finally my ministry—I mean His ministry—is beginning. I've never seen an outpouring of God like this before," Mary muses. "It's incredible! At His very words demons flee, blind eyes are opened and lepers are cleansed. Thousands are being healed. He is the King of the Jews. It was prophesied. I didn't make this up. The angel Gabriel visited me, it has all happened like he said. The excitement of the crowds grows daily as my Son walks among the people bringing revival. But what does He mean, 'Who is my mother?'"

Our greatest enemy is ourselves. It is very hard not to desire position, glory and people to revere our name. But God wants those who are concerned with the fame of His name. Mary, even as the birth mother of Jesus, had to relinquish all rights over her Son in the midst of watching the prophetic promises that were spoken over her finally be fulfilled.

After thirty years of a secret history of protecting her child, bearing the shame and stigma of His birth, and having to sacrifice her home and family only to live thirty years in obscurity preparing Jesus for this time, Mary truly had much to die to. It didn't matter what she thought she deserved or was entitled to. She had to die to even the reputation of being His mother.

God is raising up a nameless, faceless generation who will bear the mark of the cross. When people see them, they will see Jesus. An army of God is arising, ones who love not their own lives unto death. We must relinquish control and just follow the Father, even as Jesus did. This journey will take us to the cross.

It is important to realize that here Mary was in a season of blessing where the Holy Spirit was sweeping through the land by the touch of her Son. But even in this season of prosperity, God was asking that she would decrease so that He could increase.

The cycles of the prophetic carry us through a journey of increase and decrease. What season are you in? The hardest time to grow in humility is actually in seasons of great visibility and prosperity. Suffering often protects us from self-promotion and pride. Can you keep humble even in times of great blessing and increase? Can you give up control and follow Him?

Prayer: *I want to be part of Your nameless, faceless army who is desperate for Your Glory alone. Help me to relinquish my rights, die to my reputation and just follow after You.*

Day 26 – Mary's Prophetic Journey: The Dark Night of the Soul

John 19:25

Near the cross of Jesus stood his mother, his mother's sister, Mary the wife of Clopas, and Mary Magdalene.

The disciples fled to save their lives. Mary was kneeling in the shadow of the cross, weeping, screaming in anguish as her first-born Son hung naked and bloody. The ominous thunder was crowded out by Jesus' agonizing cry, "My God, My God, why have You forsaken Me?"

Mary sobs, "Why God, why? Why have You forsaken Him? Why have You forsaken me? He was supposed to deliver all of us. He was our salvation and now He's gone. If You really loved us why would You allow this?"

Mary's anguished heart bled under the shadow of a Roman cross, powerless to intervene. Her Son and her prophetic promises were dying. She had no revelation of the resurrection. She couldn't see the raging demonic battle as Jesus, the mighty warrior, snatched the keys of Death and Hell by the power of His shed blood. After waiting for thirty-three years, everything was dying—it looked like complete and utter failure.

With Jesus in the prime of His life and in the midst of a tremendous revival, He's dying on the cross—and so is Mary. She was in a crisis of faith and the Father had turned His face away. She was devastated and felt abandoned and betrayed.

The cross is being worked in our lives, sometimes even through other people's choices. When Jesus chose to go to the cross, Mary was compelled to be there too. Do you have a daughter who has had an abortion or abuses drugs? Did your dreams of a beautiful marriage end in divorce? Is your husband addicted to online pornography? Or have you felt the devastation of a child preceding you in death?

Are you in a mid-life crisis? Mary was in her late forties when her whole world caved in. We want to believe the Lord will rescue us at the last moment but often His plan is to crucify us. Everything dies at the cross: your relationships, ministry, agendas, reputation, finances—stripped bare for all to see. No one dies gracefully.

As you hit bottom, you hear the tormenting voice of the enemy whispering, "Your life is almost over and you have nothing to show for it. Where is your God now?" But as God takes you through these hot purifying fires, He works gold in the depth of your being. He gives you a love that can't be quenched by despairing circumstances. *The challenge in these times is to really believe in the goodness of God; will you believe that He is truly good, specifically to you?*

If you desire to be part of the Bride, then you need to be identified with the sufferings of the cross. In the midst of great agony and pain, when no one is there, Jesus holds you. A deeper intimacy of bridal love takes place as you cling to Him during horrendous times of suffering. We all need to cry out in total surrender, "Lord, I have no where to go. You're my all in all."

Prayer: Lord, I embrace Your cross! Father, search me and help me to nail everything—even that which You have promised me—to the cross and to let You do whatever You have to do to make me nothing less than Your reflection. Don't stop, Lord. I want all of You, so take all of me!

Day 27 – Mary's Prophetic Journey: Resurrection

Luke 24:31-34

Then their eyes were opened and they knew Him; and He vanished from their sight. And they said to one another, "Did not our heart burn within us while He talked with us on the road, and while He opened the Scriptures to us?" So they rose up that very hour and returned to Jerusalem, and found the eleven and those who were with them gathered together saying, "The Lord is risen indeed..."

Jumping up and down with ecstatic joy, the two disciples burst into the room yelling, "He's alive! He's risen!"

"When I heard those words, my heart nearly burst as I ran to see for myself. I thought I had cried all my tears on Golgotha but when our eyes met, it was like a flood. As I ran into His open arms, He scooped me up and spun me around in joyous laughter."

"Those times we shared were the most precious of my whole life. That made it easier to release Him—again. As I watched Him ascend, I prayed again, 'Lord, be it unto me as You will, for the rest of my life.'"

Out of great death comes great life! Mary's prophetic promises were limited by her worldview. She saw Jesus as King of the Jews over the little nation of Israel during her life. In reality He was King of Kings and Lord of Lords for all people, for all time. At the cross He crucifies our limited view concerning the fulfillment of our prophetic destiny and resurrects it to His eternal view. The Lord revives broken dreams but they rarely look as we expect.

"Explosions of glory! The tangible presence of the Holy Spirit! Now it was not just me who was overshadowed but all one hundred twenty of us. Tongues of fire fell and we were gloriously baptized in the Holy Spirit. We couldn't keep the news to ourselves, so we ran, pushing each other out the door and down the narrow staircase to tell everyone."

"We were so excited that we gave ourselves to prayer night and day, sharing all we had, and loving each other so much. We grew from one hundred twenty to three thousand to five thousand! Signs, wonders and miracles followed as we told everyone about Jesus. It should be easy to grow the Church until we see Jesus coming again in the clouds."

They were baptized in the Holy Spirit and the Church was set ablaze—just like the Lord wants your life to be ignited now. They received the gift of tongues and the courage to be radical and passionate lovers of Jesus Christ. The outpouring of the Holy Spirit was, and still is, a ministry of multiplication, intimacy and partnership.

When the Holy Spirit moves through you, it's not just for your benefit, but it's to bring conviction, salvation, healing and deliverance to suffering humanity. Mary was a carrier of the glory of God. Are you willing to be a carrier to bring the glory to your family, neighborhood and workplace? Are you willing to birth revival?

It was anything but easy for Mary and the early Church. Martyrdom and persecution scattered the Believers, resulting in the spread of the Gospel to other nations. Mary's journey on Earth continued not only with revival but also with seasons of tremendous warfare, cycles of life and death maturing her toward bridal love.

Prayer: Lord, thank You that You resurrect our promises so much bigger than anything we could ever imagine. Thank You that when the seed falls to the ground and dies, You bring forth a harvest of righteousness and peace. You shatter our expectations with Your goodness. I love you, Jesus.

Day 28 – Knowing the Times and the Seasons

Jeremiah 23:16, 18, 22

This is what the Lord Almighty says: "Do not listen to what the prophets are prophesying to you; they fill you with false hopes. They speak visions from their own minds, not from the mouth of the Lord... but which of them has stood in the counsel of the Lord to see or to hear His word? Who has listened and heard his word... but if they had stood in My counsel, they would have proclaimed My words to My people and would have turned them from their evil ways and from their evil deeds."

Since 9/11 we are dealing with the fear that at any moment another city in America, or maybe our city, could have limited nuclear, biological or chemical warfare. Do you ever wonder what buses are safe for your children to ride, which malls to shop at, which airplanes to take or even if it's safe to open your mail? It's essential that we hear God in these perilous times.

In addition to terrorism, there is renewed fear of financial shaking, a stock market collapse, unemployment, fuel shortages and the terrible concerns of seeing our sons and daughters on the front lines of raging wars. It is feasible that in the next decade America could move into martial law, a single world government, one world religion, and one worldwide financial system. We might trade our personal and national freedoms for global peace as the fear of evil alliances and the Antichrist loom in the future.

When another city in America is attacked—and it surely will be—great fear will sweep our nation again. It's no longer business as usual; we are moving into a season of war. It will be the best of times and the worst of times as we move closer to the end of time. Judgments are coming to the nations as the Lord shakes everything that hinders a love relationship with Him. It will be the greatest harvest of souls, accompanied with signs and wonders, yet it will be the greatest time of catastrophic bloodshed and loss.

Beloved, it is not enough to just be on the prophetic e-mail lists, to regurgitate another prophet's words, and to be an echo instead of a voice. Rather than just relying on gleaning information from newspapers, God wants you to be able to turn to Him to know what is going on in the world. We must be a people who stand in the counsels of the Lord, who know the hour and the season in which we live, and prophesy the true word of the Lord.

Prayer: *Lord, make me an Issachar prophet who would know the hour and the season in which we live. I don't want to have to read a newspaper to know what is going on, I want to hear You, know You and declare Your heart to Your people.*

Day 29 – Shaking Everything that Can Be Shaken

Haggai 2:7

"I will shake all nations, and the desired of all nations will come, and I will fill this house with glory," says the Lord Almighty.

What must we do in this hour to prepare? How do you practically prepare for the end-time calamities prophesied in the Bible? There is a holy invitation over this hour—a hand-designed, God-initiated and -written invitation to respond rightly to His desire to accelerate the work that He is doing in this hour.

The church has had 2000 years of teaching, and yet the Bride still has not made herself ready. What must we do in this hour to see the Joel two latter-day outpouring and the release of the seven-fold Spirit of Isaiah 11? We do not need more information, but impartation, because extreme times call for extreme measures. We are living in momentous days as God is preparing the Earth for a mighty visitation of His presence and His power. As we just discussed, this new season will be marked by shakings in the political, economic and natural arenas.

With the world theater teetering on the brink of World War III, God doesn't want to merely shake external infrastructures (Haggai 2), He wants to shake *you* to bring about the fullness of your destiny. Today the Lord is releasing the Isaiah seven-fold Spirit. "The Spirit of the Lord shall rest upon Him, the Spirit of wisdom and understanding, the Spirit of counsel and might, the Spirit of knowledge and of the fear of the Lord (Isaiah 11:2)." The Spirit will empower you to be a history-maker. But we have to cry out to the Lord for an empowering of his Spirit so that we can be like that temple in Haggai two—filled with His glory!

If we will make His Presence our passion and purpose in our hearts to be ready, we can stand steadfast and unshaken even in the midst of end-time tribulations. The Lord is opening supernatural treasure and provision from Heaven based upon the choices that His people are making. Activate your will now to align with God's! The cry of our heart has to be for God's Kingdom to come and His will to be done on Earth as it is in Heaven.

Then when the nations rage, evil world rulers plot in vain and people are confused at world events, we can stand confident and calm, knowing who our God is!

Prayer: *God, I want to be a history-maker! Shake everything that can be shaken in me. I don't want a religious routine, rather I want the high adventure of a being a radical forerunner who will gladly give up all for You. Fill me with Your glory to touch this world for Jesus!*

Day 30 – Dead Men Walking

Luke 9:23-24

If anyone desires to come after Me, let him deny himself, and take up his cross daily, and follow Me. For whoever desires to save his life will lose it, but whoever loses his life for My sake will save it.

Revelation 12:11

Many will lose their lives and be martyred, but they will overcome their accuser by the blood of the Lamb and by the word of their testimony, not having loved their lives to the death.

I once saw a pastor standing in front of a large world map that was mounted on the wall of his church. The Holy Spirit was brooding over the room. In tears, he told the Lord that he would send his sons and daughters from his church to the nations—even if it meant that they would be martyred. Child of destiny, release your life to the glorious cause of Christ. Learn to love Him so much that you, too, will join those who have not loved their lives to the death.

From Yearning to Burning!

Many of us sit in dead, dull churches week after week, longing to do radical exploits and move in signs and wonders... but we don't. We yearn to be ablaze with something worth dying for, something that would so grip and move our hearts that we would soar above the mundane and the pettiness of this world. Yet, many of us do not even walk across the street to witness to our lost and dying neighbors.

How do we get from yearning to burning? We need what the men and women of old possessed... a revelation of His majesty and incomprehensible love so that our testimony cannot be stopped, no matter what the circumstances are.

Visitation brings Revelation!

We all long to be burning and shining lamps like John the Baptist, with the fire of Holy Spirit blazing within our being. He received a revelation of the Bridegroom King and did not love his life, even unto death. How we need a visitation from the Beautiful One—a visitation and revelation that so rocks the core of our being that nothing stays the same. Go or stay... live or die... plenty or nothing... we would desire only one thing—to run with Him.

Prayer: Lord, I want to decrease that You might increase! Help me to be crucified with Christ so that it is no longer I who lives but Christ who lives in me! I want to be a dead man walking—one the enemy cannot kill because I am already dead to everything but Christ. Take all of me so that I can have all of You.

Day 31 – Martyrdom:
Their Blood Cries Out

Rev. 12:10-11

Then I heard a loud voice saying in Heaven "Now salvation, and strength, and the Kingdom of our God, and the power of His Christ have come, for the accuser of our brethren, who accused them before our God day and night, has been cast down." And they overcame him by the blood of the Lamb and by the word of their testimony, and they did not love their lives to the death.

Beaten and Raped For the Gospel

In the summer of 1998, a young woman from Sudan, Africa, was attacked, severely beaten and raped by Muslim extremists simply because she was wearing a cross. When she tried to escape, her throat was slit and she was bayoneted in the back.

Her assailants ripped her dress off and proceeded to melt water bottles and pour the hot, liquid plastic onto her skin, leaving it in puddles and scarring her for life. She survived the brutal assault, only to become pregnant by the horrible incident, and is now raising her child.

600 Million Suffering People

Seventy-five percent of the world's Christians live in third-world nations—nations that are predominantly Hindu, Buddhist and Muslim. Persecution in many nations brings extortion, family division, harassment and discrimination in employment and education, while over 600 million Christians live as second-class citizens in their societies.

Pacifying Theology

In the Western Church today, "intimacy with Jesus" has become a sweet and oft-heard phrase echoing in church halls as Believers quote Philippians 3:10, "That I may know Him and the power of His resurrection..." without finishing the verse, "...and the fellowship of His sufferings, being conformed to His death."

This irony is a powerful revelation—intimacy comes through suffering! That is why Holy Spirit chose to use Paul not only to pen these words, but also to demonstrate them through his own life of suffering for the Gospel.

The Western Church has developed the pacifying theology that suffering is not the will of God, but that it is Satan wreaking havoc in the life of a Believer. However, accusations in our hearts about God's inability to alleviate pain and suffering in our lives will prevent us from embracing the Cross. If we truly want to be one who is a Bride fit for her Husband, we must be willing to do that which He did: lay down our lives for the sake of love.

Prayer: Lord, I want to give You my life no matter what the cost. Teach me to love not my life even unto death. Even as You died for me, help me to be willing to die for You. You are worth everything I have. So all I am, my past, present and future, is at the foot of Your cross. Take all of me.

CHAPTER IV

The Father, Son and Holy Spirit Desire...

W. Lynn Furrow

*W. Lynn Furrow is the founder and director of
Inheritance Ministries, a ministry dedicated to seeing
the Church truly become the inheritance and the reward
for which Christ suffered, a Bride reflecting the glory and
the beauty of Jesus. It is Lynn's desire to communicate the
Word from a God-centered perspective that challenges the
Church to enter into greater maturity, intimacy and
whole-hearted passion for the Lord.*

*Lynn has been involved in both church-planting and
pastoral ministry for the last nineteen years in Minnesota,
Wisconsin and Indiana. He has also traveled overseas a
number of times, having a specific burden for the nations
of Nigeria and Argentina. Currently, he is engaged in a
church-planting initiative in the Indianapolis metropolitan
area. Lynn and his wife, Karmen, are also involved in
raising up the Indianapolis House of Prayer.*

*Lynn travels throughout the Midwest providing oversight
for several churches, ministering at conferences, and
teaching at schools of ministry for local churches in order
to equip and release the saints for the work of the
Kingdom.*

*Lynn and Karmen currently reside in Pendleton, Indiana,
with their six children.*

*For more information, please e-mail Lynn at
wlfur@aol.com.*

Day 1 – Living Before an Audience of One

1 Kings 17:1

And Elijah the Tishbite, of the inhabitants of Gilead, said to Ahab, "As the Lord God of Israel lives, before whom I stand, there shall not be dew nor rain these years, except at my word."

From seemingly complete hiddenness and obscurity, Elijah burst forth onto the pages of Scripture. In this first mention of his life, we are introduced not to a great prophet or intercessor for Israel, but to a simple inhabitant from an obscure village. However, this unknown man fearlessly confronts a wicked king by releasing a prophetic word that would shut the heavens and lead to the return of a backslidden nation.

Where did this man get such boldness and power? The secret of Elijah's power and anointing is found in his words to Ahab, "As the Lord God of Israel lives, before whom I stand..." The reality of living his life in the light of an eternal God had come to totally dominate and shape his perspective. He was free from the fear of man and the compromising spirit that allows a man to exist, but never truly be God's alone.

In this hour, the Church must renew her vision to see those things which are unseen and be moved by the One who is invisible. Only then will she have the spiritual authority and power to confront the prevailing powers of our day and turn wayward nations back to the living God. We must once again discover the power of a life lived before an audience of One.

Prayer: Oh eternal Father, would You restore the sight of Your Bride to see those things that are invisible? Would You allow the reality of eternity to break into our everyday lives? Let the weight of Heaven be brought to bear upon us so that we would live our lives in the awe and fear of who You are. Awaken us from the slumber of familiarity with the natural things that surround us. Let us see Your glory and majesty, oh living, holy One.

Day 2 – God's Provision: Lessons in Humility

1 Kings 17:9

Arise, go to Zarephath, which belongs to Sidon, and dwell there. See, I have commanded a widow there to provide for you.

Living before the Lord means that, if we are to experience the provision He has for us, we must follow His leading wherever He directs us. However, the ways God provides for His servants can often be a humbling experience. Many times God leads us to seek provision from sources where profound lack already exits. God did not send Elijah to a wealthy king, a businessman or a benefactor to sustain him during this time of drought and famine. The Lord directed Elijah to a Gentile widow that had only enough food to feed herself and her son one final meal. Can you imagine yourself in Elijah's shoes? Can you imagine asking this widow to share her last stock of food, literally taking food from her starving child's mouth to give it to a stranger? Are you willing to receive God's provision for your life from those whose own need is greater than yours? If we are unwilling to humble ourselves to receive from the source God has chosen for us, we may miss the greater miracle of provision that God is at work doing.

The truth in Elijah's case was that God wanted not only to provide for Elijah, but also to save and preserve a widow and her son from slowly dying of starvation. Elijah's request for food required boldness, but it also required an even greater humility. The prophet's humble request invited the widow to release what she had so that God could release a greater supply—more than enough for them all!

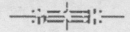

Prayer: Father, You have cared and provided for us in such marvelous ways. Continue to deepen our dependence upon Your voice. Show us where You desire to release Your provision for us and where deliverance can be released through us.

Day 3 – Praying Prayers
That Could Hurt You

James 5:17

Elijah was a man with a nature like ours, and he prayed earnestly that it would not rain: and it did not rain on the land for three years and six months.

Most of us change only when we hurt enough that we have to. This becomes a spiritual dilemma for every intercessor who desires true transformation of those for whom he is praying. Sometimes the only prayers that are left to pray for a wayward individual or nation are prayers like the one Elijah prayed. Elijah proceeded to ask God to shut the heavens, knowing that the answer to his prayer would mean a devastating famine that would endanger his own life.

In this hour, are we willing to say to God, "Do whatever it takes," even if *whatever it takes* means that the answer to our desperate cry is the disruption of our own comfort and convenience? According to Scripture, Elijah's nature and feelings were just like ours. During the three and a half years of this prayer-induced famine, Elijah experienced the pain of his answered prayer to see a nation restored and returned to their God. True revival and the transformation of our families, cities and nations will not come until we are willing to pray prayers that could hurt us.

Prayer: *Father, we desire to see true renewal and transformation in our families and our nation. Oh Spirit of God, give us Your heart that we might intercede with the heart of the true Intercessor, Christ Jesus. Give to us a willingness to sacrifice our own wellbeing and comfort to see change come to our land. Father, we say, "Whatever it takes!"*

Day 4 – Confidence and Character Birthed from Controversy

1 Kings 18:17

Then it happened, when Ahab saw Elijah, that Ahab said to him, "Is that you, oh troubler of Israel?"

A life of obedience to God means a life of controversy and confrontation. Elijah's obedience to prophesy that there would be no rain caused him to be caught in a swirl of controversy and misunderstanding. His willingness to confront King Ahab had been for the restoration of Israel, but now after more than three years of drought, it looked as if his prophetic action had been for destruction instead salvation. Needless to say, he now found himself as the most unpopular and misunderstood man alive.

Elijah, in radical obedience, risked his life only to earn the inauspicious title of "Troubler of Israel," not "Deliverer of Israel". Surely the people of God should have understood what motivated him to take such a drastic action!

Usually when we step into new levels of obedience, things get worse before they get better. However, it is in the crucible of misunderstanding that our motivations for obedience are purified, and God's voice can be heard whispering to us to persevere in patient, quiet confidence until the purpose for our obedience is clearly seen.

Prayer: *Father, Your ways are past finding out, but we still cry, "Teach us Your ways!" We accept the cup of misunderstanding as part of a life of true of obedience. Help us to respond to these tests in a way that glorifies You.*

Day 5 – It's Time to Decide

1 Kings 18:21

And Elijah came to all the people, and said, "How long will you falter between opinions? If the Lord is God, follow Him; but if Baal, follow him."

Before the Lord can disclose to us the fullness of Himself, He must have all of us. That is why when His Bride has a divided, wandering and wayward heart, the God whose name is Jealous will always bring His beloved to the crossroads of a decision. The author of Hebrews describes God as a "consuming fire" (Hebrews 12:1). His desire and longing for His people will not be satisfied until His burning heart has consumed all other lesser gods. Our Bridegroom King will not share us with another. He will have all of us or none of us.

In this hour, the Bride of Christ is being brought into the valley of decision. And here the Lord is asking us the same simple question that He, through Elijah, asked the children of Israel. "How long will you falter between opinions? If the Lord is God, follow Him; but if Baal, follow him."

When God asks you a question, not answering is not an option. He will have our decision on record. What will you decide?

Prayer: Lord Jesus, I confess now that my heart is prone to wander. Oh Burning Heart, consume me with Your fiery love! Inflame my heart with a love for You and You alone. In this hour we say, "God will be our God and we shall be His people!"

Day 6 – The God Who Answers by Fire, He is God!

1 Kings 18:24

Then you call on the name of your gods, and I will call on the name of the Lord; and the God who answers by fire, He is God.

Why fire? When you have been in a three and a half-year drought, if you want to be the spiritual hero you say, "The God who answers by rain, He is God." It would seem logical that the same God who caused the rain to cease could prove His supremacy of power by turning the rain back on. However, the culmination of this prophetic scenario was not about meeting the felt needs of the children of Israel so that their lives in the Promised Land could return to normal. When God works a miracle it is always a means to His end. He is the one who chooses the means by which He will reveal what He longs for.

Yes, superficially Israel needed rain to break the drought, but their real need was for fire back on their altar. In Leviticus 6:13, God had commanded Israel, "A fire shall always be burning on the altar; it shall never go out." God had originally supplied Israel with fire from Heaven for their altar, but they were instructed to feed the flame. The fire represented God's abiding holy presence with His covenant people. Israel had been commissioned to be the keeper of that flame. God's presence in their midst was the sign that the Lord was uniquely the God of Israel and Israel was uniquely His people. Their neglect of the flame had caused them to let the fire be extinguished, and if there is no fire, there is no need for an altar; if there is no need of an altar, there is no need for worship; if there is no worship, there is no intimacy of relationship. No, God was not going to send a thunderstorm. He was going to show that He wanted His sons and daughters back! He was going to light up the sky with a consuming fire so hot that it would devour everything it touched, just to let a lost nation know that the God of Israel was consumed with a burning jealousy and a fiery love that could not be quenched by their neglect or indifference. God would get their attention with a drought but He would reclaim them, not with water, but with holy fire!

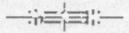

Prayer: *Consuming Fire, we desire Your presence to return to the altar. We say that it is Your presence that has distinguished us as the people of God. More than the air we breathe and the food we eat, we long for Your manifest presence. Return to Your house with fire—holy fire!*

Day 7 – Go Ahead, Give it Your Best Shot!

1 Kings 18:25

Now Elijah said to the prophets of baal, "Choose one bull for yourselves and prepare it first, for you are many; and call on the name of your god, but put no fire under it."

One of the great burdens of the Church in our generation should be to vindicate the great name of our God. His name is dishonored, reviled, blasphemed and taken in vain on a regular basis. So our cry should be, "When, Lord, will You show Your strength as You have done in days of old? Reveal Your holy right arm of power and let the world know who You really are!" However, God seems to prefer to let His challengers go first. He seems to enjoy the drama of letting His adversaries have every advantage, prospering in their conspiracies and gathering influence over more and more people and nations. But rest assured, He is only setting the stage to demonstrate the impotency of the imposters who opposed Him and to vindicate His great and holy name with signs and wonders. Our mission, then is to stay out of God's way and let Him set the stage for His own vindication. However, He does allow us the privilege of bringing this word of encouragement to His enemies, "Go ahead and give it your best shot."

The psalmist said, "Wait on the Lord, and keep His way, and He shall exalt you to inherit the land; when the wicked are cut off you shall see it. I have seen the wicked in great power, and spreading himself like a native green tree. Yet he passed away, and behold he was no more; indeed I sought him, but he could not be found (Psalm 37:34-36)."

Prayer: *Father, many times we see the wicked prosper while the righteous are oppressed. But we will wait on You. We trust in Your mercy and justice. You will not be silent forever, but will scatter Your enemies and vindicate Your holy name. In our generation, we cry, "Show us Your strength as You have done before!"*

Day 8 – Repairing the Altar of the Lord

1 Kings 18:30

Then Elijah said to all the people, "Come near to me." So all the people came near to him, and he repaired the altar of the Lord that was broken down.

Most of us would think that after hours of waiting and watching the futile efforts of the priests of Baal, Elijah would have hurriedly prepared the sacrificial offering to bring about the conclusion of a long and exhausting day. Instead, Elijah began a tedious and methodical process of preparation.

The Scriptures do not tell us whether the altar was in this condition (broken down) due to neglect or physical violence, but we do know there could be no sacrifice made that day unless the altar of the Lord was restored. The altar provided the foundation for the sacrificial offering. In a prophetic act, Elijah repaired the altar by selecting twelve stones. Each stone represented one of the twelve tribes of Israel. As a whole, the altar represented the restored prophetic identity of the people of God—an identity that had been lost due to Israel's complacency and compromise.

As Elijah set each stone in place to restore the altar, his actions were prophetically revealing the Father's heart towards the sons and daughters of Israel. The Lord was using the prophet to say to Israel that Jehovah would reveal Himself by fire only in response to an act of true worship. Furthermore, no worship or sacrifice could take place unless the altar, which represented their spiritual identity, was restored. God was not going to respond to Elijah's offering just to prove that He was the true God. God does not have to prove His existence to anyone! God was going to answer by fire, so that a lost generation could recapture their lost identity.

In this hour, the Church is frantically engaged in the hustle and bustle of religious activity and sacrifice, but still, there is no fire from Heaven. Our problem is not in the quantity of our sacrificial offerings, but upon what our worship is based. The altar of the Church's true identity is lying in ruins. Where are the Elijahs of God who will begin to repair the altar of the Lord in our day and help the Church recapture her lost identity?

Prayer: *Father, Your Church's identity has been lost in our generation. Give us wisdom to reclaim the stones of truth that will restore the lost identity of Your people. We will not rush to sacrifice until Your altar is restored. Give us wisdom so that we can build a true foundation for true worship. Strengthen our hands for this good work.*

Day 9 – Israel Shall Be Your Name

1 Kings 18:31

And Elijah took twelve stones, according to the number of the tribes of the sons of Jacob, to whom the word of the Lord had come, saying, "Israel shall be your name."

The origin of Israel's identity had come from the Lord Himself. He had called and drawn a people to Himself for the distinct purpose of disclosing Himself to them. In Exodus 19:5-6, the Lord revealed to Israel His desire for them. This scripture says, "You shall be a peculiar treasure unto Me: for all the Earth is Mine. You shall be unto Me a kingdom of priests, and a holy nation."

Israel's identity was created and shaped by their unique responsibility as stewards of the knowledge of the glory of God. He would take Israel as an inheritance for Himself, and in turn would give Himself solely unto them, clothing them with His glory and truth. God would name them for Himself thus giving birth to a new nation with a new identity. This new identity would become the birthplace of true worship in the Earth. Man would no longer worship on an altar of his own making, or devise a god after his own imagination. Israel would be a city set upon a hill, a light to the nations, bringing revelation of the knowledge of the glory of God to the people of the Earth through their worship of the only true and living God.

Like Israel, the Church must retrace her steps down ancient paths to rediscover the place of true worship. We must re-examine the foundation upon which we are presently worshiping. The rediscovery of our true identity will only be found in the intimate knowledge of who God is and who we are to Him. Out of the wellspring of these truths, we will once again secure our identity and return unto the One who has called us by name.

———:ון≡╪≡ון:———

Prayer: Abba, You have called us by name. We are Yours and Yours alone. We have no identity or destiny outside of that which You have purposed for us in You. We are Your inheritance, Your reward! We desire that a new birth of worship would arise within Your church in this hour so You can clothe us with the glory You have longed to bestow upon us before the foundations of the world. Father, we desire to be the worthy reward for which Your Son suffered, an inheritance that is filled with the glory and beauty of Christ Jesus.

Day 10 – Identity:
The Foundation of Destiny

1 Kings 18:32a

Then with the stones he built an altar in the name of the Lord.

Elijah reconstructed the altar of the Lord, which represented recapturing the prophetic identity of the nation of Israel. Just as preparation of the altar preceded the sacrifice, so must rediscovery of the church's identity precede the fulfillment of her destiny. Our destiny is fire and glory, but God will not entrust fire and glory to just anyone. We must make sure that we are using the stones and building blocks the Lord has provided for the altar that He is building in our generation.

Identity can mean, "the distinctive character or likeness that belongs to an individual, making that person unique, and directly relates to their purpose." In Genesis we see how God provided the basis of man's unique identity for him. Genesis 1:27 says, "So God created man in His own image; in the image of God He created him." God created man with a divine imprint of His own image; this made humans distinct from every other created thing. God desired to use this divine imprint to lead man into an ever-deepening relationship with Himself. As man continued to fellowship and commune with his Creator, a greater sense of identity and purpose could begin to form. Ultimately, it was in God's heart to cultivate such a deep relationship with Adam and Eve that He could fully disclose Himself to them, and they could enjoy the pleasure of knowing God for eternity.

Yet when Adam and Eve chose to willingly disobey God, they embarked on a path of deception that led them to attempt to establish their own identity and destiny apart from God. They believed they could still relate to God on their own terms. They would sacrifice, but on an altar of their own choosing.

For thousands of years now mankind has built altars of intellect, power and wealth in an attempt to somehow establish meaning, significance and purpose for his life. In a perverted sense, we have tried to offer these as a sacrifice to God, declaring that now man is worthy of God's acceptance. However, the penetrating words of Jesus are still true. "The flesh profits nothing (John 6:23)." Nothing? Do we really believe this? Man is so ingenious, enterprising and creative, surely there is an altar he could build that could be a true foundation of worship. But again the words of Jesus bring finality to the efforts of man to fulfill his destiny by himself. He said, "Without Me you can do nothing (John 15:5)."

Prayer: *Lord Jesus, Your Word is truth. We boldly confess that without You we can do nothing. Teach us to lean more and more upon Your breast, our Beloved. We desire that our life and identity be hidden in You and You alone. "Less of us and more of You," is our cry.*

Day 11 – Stones of Identity: The Intimate Knowledge of His Pleasure, Purpose and Will

Ephesians 1:9

Having made known to us the mystery of His will, according to His good pleasure which He purposed in Himself.

Just as Elijah used stones as building blocks for the altar, the Lord has specific truths to give us to restore the altar of the Church's identity in our generation. The basis of our identity is the intimate knowledge of who God is and what He has purposed for us in Him.

In Ephesians 1:9, the apostle Paul breaks down the revelation of God's personhood into three distinct components: His pleasure, His purpose and His will. His *good pleasure* can be defined as what pleases Him. What are the longings of His heart? His *purpose* is the resolute intention of God to fulfill His own desires. Have no doubt about it; God will get what He wants. His *will* is the predetermined course of action that He will take to fulfill His purpose and gratify the longings of His heart. To understand the purpose for which we have been created, we must explore the longings that existed in God's heart before the foundations of the world. What motivated Him to create Heaven and Earth? Why was it in the predetermined counsel of God for Christ to be slain? All these questions are answered when we understand what He desires. And as we yield our lives to these longings, and surrender our will to the way in which He has determined for these desires to be fulfilled, so will we realize our true identity in Him.

Prayer: *Oh Eternal God, reveal to us what You have longed for since before the beginning of time. My perspective is so limited to my own wants and needs. Would You pull back the veil and disclose Your heart to us? We marvel at Your handiwork, Your creativity and Your genius, but what motivated You to do all that we see? Spirit of wisdom and revelation, bring understanding to us that we may know the mystery of Your will, that in ages past was hidden, but now may be known by all of mankind.*

Day 12 – The Hope of His Calling: The Father's Inheritance of Sons and Daughters

Ephesians 1:18

The eyes of your understanding being enlightened; that you may know what is the hope of His calling, and what are the riches of the glory of His inheritance in the saints.

Before the beginning of time, before the foundations of the world were laid, the eternal Godhead deeply enjoyed the communion and fellowship that existed within Themselves. Within their intimate fellowship with each other, each part of the Godhead felt and experienced the eternal longings of the others. It became the purpose of each member of the Godhead to, in love, serve and fulfill the desires of each other's heart. Thus the eternal purpose of God was born. Whatever the cost, love would pay any price to fulfill these eternal longings.

As the Son and the Holy Spirit communed with the Father, one primary longing was felt and experienced: the Father's heart burned with desire for a large family of sons and daughters upon whom He could lavish His love. He longed to forever share His heart, throne and home with these sons and daughters, surrounding them with His glory and beauty. To express this desire for sons and daughters, He issued forth an eternal call in hope, saying, "I will be a Father to you, and you shall be My sons and daughters, says the Lord Almighty (2 Cor. 6:18)."

Because of their immeasurable love for the Father, God the Son and God the Holy Spirit were willing to empower the human race from within to respond to that call; the Father's desire for sons and daughters would be fulfilled. God the

Son would take upon human flesh revealing the Father's heart and love to mankind, and destroying that which would hinder the Father's love. The Holy Spirit would dwell within human flesh, awakening a cry within the human heart to know God intimately as Father. Their love would see to it that millions of men and women would love and honor the Father the way They Themselves loved and adored Him. Now mankind would be empowered to walk in an identity beyond that which they could ask, or think, or even *imagine*. Man would now be given the ultimate right and privilege to be called the sons and daughters of the living God.

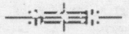

Prayer: *Oh Spirit of the living God, continue to awaken a cry of adoption in our hearts. Empower our hearts to cry out, "Abba, Father." Abba, we respond to the call that You issued forth for an inheritance of sons and daughters. We respond to Your love and we ask that You would enlarge our hearts to love You the way the Son and the Spirit love and honor You.*

Day 13 – The Longing of the Son:
The Inheritance of a Bride

Ephesians 5:30-32

For we are members of His body, of His flesh and of His bones. "For this reason, a man shall leave his father and mother and be joined to his wife, and the two shall be one flesh." This is a great mystery, but I speak concerning Christ and the Church.

Before the world was formed, it was the Father's desire to give to His Son an everlasting Kingdom and to give Him dominion over all that the Trinity would create. Just as God the Son and God the Holy Spirit felt and experienced the longing of the Father, conversely, the Father intimately knew the longing of His Son. The Son desired not just an empire, but He longed for a companion that could sit at His side, ruling and reigning with Him forever—for what is a kingdom without companionship?

So the Father determined that a suitable helpmate would be found for the eternal Son of God. In chapter five of the book of Ephesians, the apostle Paul confirms this truth, and reveals that the relationship between a husband and wife is really a prophecy that foretells of a greater eternal marriage between Christ and His Church. However, just as Adam longed for a suitable partner and none was found, the Father knew that without a special act of creation, a suitable companion would not exist for His Son. In Genesis, the first Adam was put to sleep so that a bride could be taken from his side. When God brought Eve to Adam, the man declared, "This is now bone of my bone and flesh of my flesh." In like manner, the last Adam, Christ Jesus, would have to sleep the sleep of death so that from His wounded side a Bride could be created both for Him and from Him.

The same expression is used by Paul in Ephesians 5:30, describing the mystery of the Church being Christ's Bride, saying, "For we are members of His body, of His flesh and of His bones." This miracle produced a new creation from Christ, for Christ. After searching through all of the created order without finding a suitable partner, when Adam saw his newly fashioned bride for the first time he declared, "This is it!" Like Adam, Christ beholds His Bride and declares over us, "This is the Church: a Bride, taken from My side as a new creation, then made into an equal partner that will reign with Me forever!"

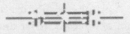

Prayer: Father, we recognize the love that You have placed in our hearts for Your Son. As His bride we declare that we love Him, but we ask that You would continue to mature our love. We give thanks for the reality of the new creation in our lives—the reality of a new bridal identity. Truly, old things have passed away and You have made everything new. We look forward with anticipation to the marriage supper of the Lamb, when finally we will see our Bridegroom King face to face.

Day 14 – The Formation of Our Bridal Identity

Ephesians 5:31-32

For this reason a man shall leave his father and mother and the two shall be one flesh. This is a great mystery, but I speak concerning Christ and the Church.

Marriage is a prophetic picture of a greater eternal union that is to come, between Christ and His Church. God also uses the same human relational process of courtship and engagement to display the bridal identity between Christ and His Church. In the natural, the marriage union is the culmination of a relational process that requires an ever-increasing degree of intimacy. Each relational stage demands greater risk and vulnerability in the hopes that it will achieve a greater level of intimacy. Every time the couple enters a new level of relating, they must commit to revealing who they really are with a greater transparency to each other. Certain feelings and secrets of the heart which at one time had to be hidden are now revealed. As this once secret and intimate knowledge is shared, and these innermost thoughts and feelings are held sacred by the other, a bond of trust begins to mature. What were once private ideas, thoughts and feelings, are now thought and felt by the partner as well. In this way these two distinct lives become ever more closely intertwined with shared experiences which lead to the possibility of the two now becoming one. This initial stage of the relational process is called courtship, and the final preparatory stage before marriage is, of course, engagement.

Paul said in 1 Cor. 15:46, "The spiritual is not first, but the natural, and afterward, the spiritual." God established the process of courtship, engagement and marriage in the natural to foreshadow and reveal to us an ongoing, unseen spiritual process of God's courtship and engagement of

200

mankind. Through the incarnation, we see God in Christ coming in courtship to engage mankind in divine romance. We see that God's desire was not just for casual friendship, but to be in covenant union with man. This is demonstrated by His willingness to share in the human experience.

I believe the purpose of the incarnation was not an attempt to fully understand man; Christ the Creator already knew everything about mankind, His creation. It was to show that He was willing to identify with humankind in their weakness, pain and sin, breaking down the barriers of fear and mistrust that reside in each individual. The incarnation was a revelation of God's perfect love so that man could be delivered from their secret fears and insecurities, free to love and trust someone other than themselves. God, revealing His love through Christ, demonstrated to mankind that, in desiring a relationship with them, His intentions were pure and they could completely trust Him. In Christ no one would ever have to be left in the desert of his own fear and loneliness. Once humanity understood the purity of God's intention towards them in courtship, they could believe and trust in the promise of an eternal union yet to come.

Prayer: *Oh beautiful God, beautiful Man Christ Jesus, You have won my heart. No one has loved me the way You love me. Divine Romancer, by the perfection of Your love, continue to deliver me from the fears that torment. Thank You for Your willingness to strip Yourself of Your glory and come to us robed in human flesh. Thank You for the cross, where You put the perfection of Your love on display for Your Bride. I will never forget it!*

Day 15 – The Longing of the Holy Spirit: The Inheritance of a Place of Rest and Expression

Isaiah 66:1

Thus says the Lord: "Heaven is My throne and Earth is My footstool. Where is the house that you will build Me? And where is the place of My rest?"

In laying the stones of truth that secure the altar of our identity, we cannot neglect the third Person of the divine Trinity. The Holy Spirit also has longings and desires that will be fulfilled in us as we yield our lives to the purpose for which we were created. The Father longs for a family, the Son longs for His Bride, but what is it that the Holy Spirit desires?

Every person desires to have the right of self-expression and to be accepted for who they are. This is why we like to go to a place we call "home." Home is a place where we can let down our guard and be ourselves. We are only truly at rest when we can be ourselves. Do we think the Holy Spirit would be any different? I believe the Holy Sprit longs to find a place of rest; He is the one member of the divine Trinity who has chosen to live within us as His dwelling place.

Can you imagine the arrogance of an individual who prepares a place for a person to live, but then denies that person the ability to be themselves? We would call that a prison, not a home. The apostle Paul warned that in the last days men would create a form and place for God, but deny Him the right of self-expression (2 Tim. 3:5). As a matter of fact, most of our structures are geared around what fits our lifestyles and preferences, what is comfortable and what is convenient to our schedules. We like a god that is made in our image and in our likeness, instead of the other way around.

Oh beloved, the Holy Spirit longs to come to the Church not just in visitation, but in habitation. He desires to dwell and find a resting place in us. Only when we permit Him to be Himself can He fully disclose and unveil to us the mystery of who He really is. What will you do to give Him a place of rest?

Prayer: *Holy Spirit, I long to give You a place of rest. Break through my limiting mindsets and attitudes. I desire that You would be able to be all that You are within me. Forgive me if I have quenched Your presence or grieved You. Have Your way and make Your resting place in me.*

Day 16 – The Father's Pleasure

Matthew 5:3

Blessed are the poor in spirit, for theirs is the Kingdom of Heaven.

The building blocks of identity consist not only of our spiritual understanding of the intimate knowledge of God (His longings, purposes and will), but also of the revelation of the provision that God has released to us so that we might become an inheritance for Him. In the Sermon on the Mount, Jesus announced the divine empowerments that would be released for those who, in their weakness and spiritual desperation, would long to enter into such a great Kingdom.

Jesus began by declaring that there is a superceding right above all the other rights—a right of rights as it were, that would explain how the other privileges would be possible for such broken people. Jesus made a radical statement, saying that the Kingdom and all that it entails would be open for everyone, and that its provision was not for some future day but was a present reality. All that Heaven encompasses is radically available for those trapped in the grip of spiritual poverty. Beloved, everything that you need to become what God longs for you to become is yours and available to you now. Jesus said, "Do not fear little flock, for it is your Father's good pleasure to give you the Kingdom (Luke 12:32)."

Prayer: Oh Father, I want to believe that everything about Your Kingdom is available to me right now. Cause faith to arise in my heart from knowing Your heart towards me. In my spiritual weakness and desperation, let me experience the present reality of Your Kingdom in my life. I want to feel Your good pleasure in giving me the Kingdom.

Day 17 – The God of All Comfort

Matthew 5:4

Blessed are those who mourn, for they shall be comforted.

When we see the state of our own spiritual poverty in comparison to the vast riches and abundance of our Father's Kingdom, we mourn over our lost, impoverished condition. We become gripped with spiritual grief when we recognize what might have been if only we could have realized our spiritual poverty earlier. Just think of all the wasted years, the broken relationships, the hurt and pain inflicted upon your heart and the hearts of others, all because we felt the need to try the vain pursuit of proving our own self-sufficiency...

But the sorrow over what has been lost can be a pathway to healing. Jesus told the compelling story of a son who, in the midst of his sorrow, realized what he had lost. When the father saw his son coming, Scripture tells us, "His father had compassion, and ran and fell on his neck and kissed him (Luke 15:20)." The father did not speak a word but gave his broken son the only active medicine for mourning: comfort. The father's kiss and embrace communicated more in a moment than millions of words could have communicated in a lifetime. This acceptance let a grieving son know that no matter where he had been or what had happened, he was home now... it was going to be okay. Oh beloved, if you are in mourning over what has been lost, run into the arms of your Father. He is the God of all comfort.

Prayer: *Oh Father, I have squandered divine chances by complaining about my difficulties and closing my heart to the pain. Touch my heart and speak Your word to my spirit. I know that just one word from You can bring life and comfort to me.*

Day 18 – The God of Prosperity

Matthew 5:5

Blessed are the meek, for they shall inherit the Earth.

When we think of the Kingdom of God, we tend to think of it as somewhere "out there." We think of God's Kingdom existing only in a spiritual dimension and then there is this natural realm where we live. We think of them as separate creations. However, the spiritual and the natural realms are simply two dimensions of one creation. So God's Kingdom does not exist any less in the natural realm than it does in the spiritual. That is why if it is all God's creation, then it is all an expression of the King's domain whether in the natural or the spiritual; He created it and He owns it. Therefore because of the seamlessness between the realms, I believe God is very interested in "real estate," and even more importantly, who owns it. Allow me to explain what I mean.

God has determined that this planet and everything it contains be given as an inheritance to His Son and those who are in covenant relationship with Him. The full extent of that inheritance may not be realized by the sons and daughters of the King until His return, but in every aspect of our redemption there is a foreshadowing of the reality of the age to come. We should not be shocked then to see that one of the purposes of the Church, as authorized agents of the Kingdom in the Earth, is the creation of wealth. And the purpose of the power to create wealth is to demonstrate to those still outside the covenant the reality of that covenant and the King who made it; wealth gained through covenant showcases the God who gave it. Deuteronomy 8:18 says, "And you shall remember the Lord your God, for it is He who gives you the power to get wealth, that He may establish His covenant." Beloved, God desires to demonstrate and further establish His Kingdom through you. So do not be surprised if the God who gives the power to get wealth comes by for a visit, because He has determined, child of the King, that you shall inherit the Earth.

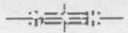

Prayer: *Lord Jesus, we acknowledge that the Earth is Yours and everything in it. We thank You for supplying all of our needs according to Your riches in glory. We thank You that You not only prosper us spiritually, emotionally and physically, but that You desire to prosper us financially. As a sign of the reality of Your covenant with us, You said that You would make us the head and not the tail, that we would be above and not beneath, and that we would be the lender and not the borrower. We humble ourselves, and in meekness we ask You to teach us Your ways, so that we can be Your covenant people.*

Day 19 – The God of Fullness

Matthew 5:6

Blessed are those who hunger and thirst for righteousness, for they shall be filled.

Not only is God determined to satisfy His own longings for an inheritance, but He is determined to satisfy us as well. His design for His royal family is that they experience fullness. What a concept! *Everything that can be known about and experienced in God is possible.*

He has purposed for us to know Him the way He knows us. Paul told the Corinthian Believers that the express role of the Holy Spirit in this age is to search and reveal, "All things, yes, the deep things of God (1 Cor. 2:10)." Did Paul say *all things*? Beloved, nothing is off limits. So enjoy the endless journey into the center of the heart of God. This journey will thrill you, delight you, satisfy you, and still leave you with the desire for more.

Prayer: *Lord, I am hungry. I have run after other things and they do not satisfy the longing in my heart. You alone can satisfy me, so draw me back with still more hunger for You. Oh Holy Spirit, reveal to me what You have searched and found—the deep things of God. I want to know and explore the vast, unending ocean of Your heart.*

Day 20 – The God of Mercy

Matthew 5:7

Blessed are the merciful, for they shall obtain mercy.

Mercy is the wellspring from which true forgiveness comes forth. Forgiveness apart from mercy is not forgiveness at all. It is an empty action, whereby one is simply refusing to retaliate for wrongs committed against them. The offender is still a debtor, forever on a blacklist of those who are now banned from fellowship with us. However, mercy puts emotion back into forgiveness.

Mercy compels and moves us to forgive. Why? Because mercy allows us to understand why offenders offend. Often times, individuals hurt and offend others because they have been hurt and offended themselves. The cycle of harm and hurt goes on and on and on until...

Mercy shows up on the scene, looks past the anger, hostility and resentment, and sees people for who they really are— weak and broken people, in need of love, acceptance and forgiveness. Oh warring Bride, arise with one of the greatest weapons in your arsenal: the mercy of God! Let the mercy that you have received flow like a river from your heart. Let mercy empower your words of forgiveness. When you reveal the God of mercy through a heart of love, you will bring healing to a jaded world.

***

Prayer: Oh God, make us warriors of Your mercy. Teach us, Holy Spirit, how to use mercy to strike terror into the hearts of Your enemy, the accuser of the brethren. Let Your mercy flow through us, the Body of Christ, to bring healing and life, drawing weak and broken hearts to You.

Day 21 – The God of Vision

Matthew 5:8

Blessed are the pure in heart, for they shall see God.

One of the greatest marvels of the new birth is the creative miracle of spiritual faculties. There are no spiritual birth defects in the Kingdom of God. In His Kingdom everyone born of God is given spiritual senses to experience the vast expanse of the height, length, width and depth of this Kingdom. Entrance into this Kingdom is the essential beginning point. Now you should begin to use your spiritual faculties to see and hear all that the Father has prepared to show you.

The natural senses you have developed will be of no use to you there. Your natural sight and hearing are much too limited to comprehend all of the things that will be shown to you (1 Corinthians 2:9). You may ask, "How, then, do these spiritual eyes work?" It all depends on what you would like to see. If you would like to see everything, you will not be able to see anything. But if you want the only necessary thing (Luke 10:41-42), you will see Him in everything.

"One thing I have desired of the Lord, that will I seek: that I may dwell in the house of the Lord all the days of my life, to behold the beauty of the Lord and to inquire in His temple (Psalm 27:4)."

Prayer: *Father of Glory, send Your Holy Spirit to anoint our eyes that we might see Your glory. Oh Father, show us Your glory! Let us behold Your beauty. Let the light of Your countenance shine upon us and let us forever be changed. Let me see through new eyes—eyes of faith that see You in every circumstance and in every situation. Give me eyes only for You!*

Day 22 – The God of Peace

Matthew 5:9

Blessed are the peacemakers, for they shall be called the sons of God.

God is the ultimate peacemaker, so it is not surprising that His children should also be peacemakers. However, the way God makes peace is quite different from the peace that the world offers. Jesus said, "Peace I leave to you, My peace I give to you; not as the world gives do I give to you (John 14:27)." God brings peace not by the outward coercion of hostile opponents, but by the release of the inward peace that exists within Himself. God can make peace because He is at peace. To put it another way, God is at peace about being God. He is confident that His purposes and plans will come to pass. There is no conflict that exists within Himself. His very being emanates a restful calm that dissipates the most violent sea or the rage of wicked men that would rise against Him.

In Psalms chapter two, the writer describes a world gone mad in violent rage and opposition to the God of Heaven. Strangely, God does not respond in the same way to them, instead He releases a laugh that reverberates through His Kingdom, once again reminding His servants of the stability of His never-ending reign. The tranquility and peace of God causes wars to cease and stabilizes the restless, fearful soul. Oh beloved, are you tossed about, facing conflicts without and within? Then let the Master of every storm-tossed sea arise within you and say, "Peace, be still."

***

Prayer: Lord Jesus, we receive the peace that only You can give. We thank You for tranquility and stability in our rough times. As Your children, make us instruments of Your peace. Amen.

Day 23 – The God of Joy

Matthew 5:11-12

Blessed are you when they revile and persecute you, and say all kinds of evil against you falsely for My name sake. Rejoice and be exceedingly glad, for great is your reward in Heaven, for so they persecuted the prophets who were before you.

God is not only concerned *that* we serve Him, but more important to Him is *how* we serve him. In Psalm 100:2, we are instructed to, "Serve the Lord with gladness." Joy and gladness should be the earmarks of our service towards the Lord. In fact, God warned Israel that they would lose their inheritance if they did not continue to serve Him with gladness (Deut. 28:47). Why are joy and gladness such defining factors of Christian service? Because to serve the Lord with gladness is to reflect the God we are serving.

Our Lord is the ultimate glad heart. On the day of His coronation as King of the Universe, when the Father invited Jesus to sit at His right hand, the Bible tells us that the anointing oil used to anoint Him as King was the oil of gladness (Hebrews 1:8-9; Psalm 45:7). This anointing of joy exceeded anyone else's in the universe. Jesus is the happiest person ever! I can only imagine what a celebration His coronation must have been. I believe that on that day our King, Glad Heart, danced like David did. That is why when we face trials and persecution, He will empower our hearts with the same anointing He is anointed with. So beloved, do you need strength for the journey? "Rejoice in the Lord always and again I will say rejoice (Phil. 4:4)!"

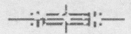

Prayer: *Oh glad-hearted King, You have been anointed with the oil of joy above every inhabitant, both in the heavens and on the Earth. Your Kingdom is a kingdom of joy. You sit upon Your throne and laugh—it terrifies Your enemies, but fills the hearts of the redeemed with strength. Your joy and gladness secure our hearts in knowing that everything You have purposed will surely come to pass. We rejoice and delight ourselves in You, oh God of our joy.*

Day 24 – Positioning Ourselves in Weakness

1 Kings 18:35

So the water ran all around the altar... and he also filled the trench with water.

In the unfolding of this prophetic drama, what Elijah did after repairing the altar and preparing the sacrifice seems quite strange. Three times Elijah had the sacrifice, the wood and the altar saturated with water. Could this prevent the sacrifice from catching on fire? Yes, but only a fire of human origin. Elijah made sure that the only fire that could be generated on that altar was fire from Heaven. He had made up his mind—no natural process would be attempted if God did not respond.

In the Church today, we must ask ourselves this question: in our life and ministries, have we positioned ourselves in sufficient weakness to the point that, unless God shows up, there will be no fire? The Church has become adept at having plenty of contingency plans if the Lord doesn't answer from Heaven. We have fire by friction, flint and steel... that flame-thrower thing worked great last time... but in this hour, we must have fire from Heaven—or no fire at all!

Prayer: Oh God of consuming fire, we confess that we have attempted to do Your work in our own strength and power. We ask that, in our weakness, You would demonstrate Your perfect strength. We are willing to be weak and foolish so that You may be shown strong. Oh God, we are desperate for Your fire—fire from Heaven! We will wait, no matter how long it takes.

Day 25 – All-Consuming Fire!

1 Kings 18:38

Then the fire of the Lord fell and consumed the burnt sacrifice, and the wood and the stones and the dust, and it licked up the water that was in the trench.

Repairing the altar and preparing a sacrifice is a lot of hard work, but wait a minute, what are we building it for? Yes, you got it right. He is going to burn it down. "You mean to tell me that all of our hard work and preparation is going to go up in smoke?" Quite frankly, yes. His fire will devour everything it touches.

This is tough for us to handle because deep down we would like to see our altar and sacrifice burning, but not consumed—something like a burning shrine that we can open up for spiritual tourists to come and see. As they pass by the glowing altar I can say, "I helped build that altar." No, when God comes with fire, everything that we have set in place to attract Him there will be consumed by that flame. The only legacy that will remain will be in the memory of the One who is the all-consuming fire.

Prayer: Father, we give to You our lives and ministries. Everything that we have done or are doing to prepare for You a place of habitation is at Your disposal. Do with it as You will. The only lasting legacy we want is that we were a part of an altar and sacrifice in our generation that was fuel for Your fire. We are willing to be consumed for Your glory. It is all for You. Yours is the Kingdom and the power and the glory.

Day 26 – The Lord, He is God!

1 Kings 18:39

Now when all the people saw it, they fell on their faces; and they said, "The Lord, He is God! The Lord, He is God!"

As the fire of the Lord fell from Heaven, the children of Israel went from standing to lying prostrate, from silence to thunderous, repeated praise. A backslidden, idolatrous nation was suddenly turned back to God in a moment. Many times we see the idolatry of our own nation and we wonder if our nation could ever return to the Lord. We feel as though the odds are insurmountable. Can anything turn the tide? We forget that the national revival recorded in 1 Kings 18 occurred because God responded to the offering of one fearless worshipper of God.

Dear one, do not think that your devotion to Jesus does not have an impact. There will be a day when the God of fire responds to your worship, and the multitudes, who just the day before were opposing God and His rule, will be on their faces declaring the glory and the majesty of the name of Jesus. All because someone saw an altar and repaired it. All because someone cried out that there must be fire upon it.

Prayer: Oh Lord Jesus, we long for the day when Your Church is clothed with Your glory; when entire cities will be shaken by Your power; when streets will be filled with new Believers singing the spontaneous praises of God for the great works You have done. But until that day comes, we will not relent in our worship and intercession. We will boldly join with the company of the few who labor in night and day prayer until You rend the heavens and come down. We will not stop crying until Your name is a praise in the entire Earth!

Day 27 – The Sound of the Abundance of Rain!

1 Kings 18:41

Then Elijah said to Ahab, "Go up, eat and drink; for there is the sound of the abundance of rain."

Do you see anything yet? The fire has returned to the altar of the Lord. Sons and daughters are turning their hearts toward the Father. Surely we should be seeing something by now. Do you see the long-awaited, unprecedented, worldwide move of God's Spirit? Have you seen miracles yet—blind eyes opened, deaf ears hearing, the lame walking, the dead raised to life again? No? Well then I will let you in on a little secret. Hearing must precede seeing. Before Elijah saw even one drop of rain or a cloud in the sky, he prophesied to King Ahab that he could hear the sound of an abundance of rain.

The real question is, "Do you hear the sound?" If you hear what I'm hearing, then prophesy, for there is going to be an abundance of rain!

Prayer: *Father, we hear the sound in our spirits. We hear the thunder roll of Your Kingdom's preparation for what You are going to do on the Earth. King of Glory, You are issuing forth Your commands to the host of Heaven and Your church in the Earth. You are setting the stage for the fulfillment of Your promise. Give us the boldness to speak what we hear. Oh living Word, use our lips to declare Your intentions and Your purpose for our generation. We declare that this is the hour; this is the day of an unprecedented, trans-generational, worldwide outpouring of Your Spirit! So be it, in Jesus' name.*

Day 28 – Big Things Come in Small Packages!

1 Kings 18:44

Then it came to pass the seventh time, that he said, "There is a cloud, small as a man's hand, rising out of the sea!"

Intercession is like childbirth. There is a progressive spiritual labor and travail that takes place to bring about the manifestation of God's purpose on the Earth. With each spiritual contraction, there is a desperate hope that it will be the last. You say to yourself, "Maybe this will be the prayer meeting that will change everything. God will rend the heavens and come down in power and glory and we will see the unprecedented move of God's Spirit for which we have prayed." Be careful. The way God answers your prayers may be quite different than the way you have imagined.

In this story Elijah had seven times placed his head between his legs in a position of labor, interceding for the breaking of the drought that gripped Israel for three and a half years. He had turned the hearts of Israel back to God and prophesied to King Ahab that he had heard the "sound of the abundance of rain." Now was the moment of truth. What would the answer to Elijah's prayer look like? Would it be the perfect storm—a gigantic hurricane with the largest rainfall, hail and winds in recorded history? No, after praying seven times, Elijah's servant reported that the answer to the prophet's prayer was no larger than a man's hand on the horizon.

Oh intercessor, would that have brought discouragement to your heart? All these years of prayer only to produce a small cloud. It is not discouraging if you see that the cloud approaching you on the horizon shrouds the coming of the God of Glory who thunders. Big things come in small packages!

Prayer: *Lord Jesus, we know that Your Kingdom will fill the entire Earth. The knowledge of Your glory will cover the Earth as the waters cover the sea. But we recognize that the beginning of Your Kingdom was in a small stable in Bethlehem. You came in hiddenness, shrouding Yourself in human flesh, concealing Your glory. You even appeared to Your disciples in a different form on the road to Emmaus after Your resurrection. You take pleasure in hiding Yourself. Teach us never to judge Your work by the sight of our eyes. Let us never despise the day of small beginnings. Do whatever You want to do, however you want to do it. We place our expectations only in You. Amen.*

Day 29 – The Elijah Task

1 Kings 18:37

Hear me, oh Lord, that this people may know that you are the Lord God, and that You have turned their hearts back to You again.

Rebuking wicked kings, pronouncing divine judgments, repairing altars, calling down fire from Heaven—this man Elijah had quite a job! Sounds pretty intriguing, but sometimes we miss the motivation of the man by being preoccupied with the signs that accompanied his ministry. I believe what motivated Elijah was a love of Jehovah and a love for His people. The covenant relationship that had existed between the two had been shattered by Israel's idolatry. As Israel drifted further and further from their God, their unique heritage, identity and destiny were only a generation away from extinction.

Could a generation be re-awakened and reclaimed? Was there anyone who would throw himself into the breach and attempt to repair it? Only if an individual would arise without fear or compromise, and provide the leadership of a spiritual patriarch and father, could it happen. He would have to stand fixed in his convictions in the midst of a generation drowning in a sea of immorality and paganism. As a spokesman for God, he would have to roar like a lion, but in the end his heart would always ache as he longed for the sons and daughters of Israel to return to the Rock from which they were hewn. This was Elijah, a prophet indeed, but most importantly, a spiritual father whose heart became the reflection of the heart of God to his generation.

In our day, we face a similar situation—a lost nation and a forsaken generation. So many are asking the same question that Elisha asked following Elijah's catching away, "Where is the Lord God of Elijah?" However, maybe our question should really be, "Where is an Elijah for God?" Will you be an Elijah?

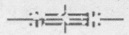

Prayer: *Father, we want to reflect Your heart, so turn our hearts toward this generation. We desire to be intercessors who will stand in the breach. God, we cry, "Give us this generation, or we die!" Hear us, oh Lord, that this generation would know that You are the Lord God, and that You have turned their hearts back to You again.*

Day 30 – Formation of Bridal Intimacy: Engagement

2 Corinthians 11:2

For I am jealous for you with a godly jealousy. For I have betrothed you to one Husband, that I may present you as a chaste virgin to Christ.

Christ in the incarnation was a revelation of God's deep desire to pursue mankind in a loving relationship. To those who respond to the revelation of His perfect love and the purity of His intention in courtship, He offers a deeper level of relationship. He now proposes to betroth them in the initial stage of a permanent, covenant relationship. Unlike today, engagement, or betrothal as it was called in biblical days, was the first step of the covenant process. When a couple became engaged, they were positionally and covenantally husband and wife, even though the relationship was not physically consummated. For this union to be broken or dissolved it required the granting of a legal bill of divorce or the death of one of the covenant partners. This can be seen with Mary and Joseph in Matthew 1:18-19. This passage demonstrates not only the legal nature of their engagement, but also their perspective of each other; Joseph was clearly Mary's husband and she was his wife.

Why then did engaged couples have to wait for the physical consummation of their union? The engagement period was a transitional stage during which the man and woman prepared themselves to fulfill the promises they made to each other when they accepted the engagement proposal. This period of time would allow them the opportunity to re-orient their thoughts, feelings and actions from those of two individuals living separate lives, to one life expressed and shared by both. The couple had to lay down their past, distinct identities and begin the process of taking upon themselves new, covenant identities. They were no longer two, but one.

For those of us who have responded to His courtship of us and accepted the engagement proposal of covenant, we are now the betrothed of the Lord. Christ Jesus views us as His bride. The apostle Paul uses this same kind of bridal language and imagery in Second Corinthians 11:2 to describe the purpose of his ministry. Paul stated, "For I am jealous for you with a godly jealousy. For I have betrothed you to one Husband, that I may present you as a chaste virgin to Christ." It is time for us now to put on this new, bridal identity and prepare ourselves to be presented to our beloved Bridegroom, Christ Jesus.

Prayer: *Oh Jesus, we want to be ready to be presented to You, clothed in Your glory and beauty. Father, have Your way in us. You know what pleases Your Son and we desire to please Him with our whole being. Please help us to understand who we really are to Your Son. We need to know our identity as His Bride. We say yes to the proposal. We say yes to our new identity. Oh Lord, make us ready for the one we love, the one who is the Lover of our souls.*

CHAPTER V

Discovering the Father's Heart

Gary Wiens

The love of the Father's heart for the Bride of Christ is the
focus of the message God is developing in the life of Gary
Wiens. An emerging joy centered in the beauty of the Lord
Jesus has given rise to a fresh passion to know Him deeply, and
to see His Bride come to her place of identity and destiny in the
knowledge of the Bridegroom. Gary's ministry is characterized
by the fiery passion of Christ's love for His Bride, the Church,
and understanding the Father heart of God.

Gary Wiens was raised, nurtured and educated in the
Mennonite Brethren denomination. After pastoring churches
in that brotherhood for seven years, he was joined to the
Vineyard movement in 1983. Gary planted the Vineyard
Christian Fellowship of Aurora, Colorado, pastoring there
for ten years, and subsequently served as the Director of Youth
Ministries at Metro Christian Fellowship in Kansas City
from July of 1996 until June 30, 1999. Since then, Gary has been
associated with Mike Bickle and the International House of
Prayer (IHOP-KC), and is now President of Burning Heart
Ministries (BHM), giving his full time in ministering to the
Lord and sharing the vision of the House of Prayer with the
Body of Christ. His commitment is to intercede over the coming
generations, and to proclaim the forerunner message so that
these generations might be drawn to their place in the Father's
purposes.

Gary now lives in Grandview, Missouri, with his children,
Dave and Steph Wiens, Alyson and Ben Alberts, and Rachel.

For more information please visit them on the web at
www.burningheartministries.com.

Day 1

Psalm 63:1-2

Oh God, You are my God; early will I seek You; my soul thirsts for You; my flesh longs for You in a dry and thirsty land where there is no water. So I have looked for You in the sanctuary, to see Your power and Your glory.

There is a longing at the bottom of the heart of every believer who is the least bit responsive to the initiatives of the Holy Spirit. Once we begin to understand that our passions were meant to be satisfied in Him, and that only in Him is found the pleasure that every person seeks, we find our focus narrowing and our options becoming few.

In these verses, the psalmist is acknowledging that there is no true enjoyment outside the presence of the Lord. He has sought for pleasure in the dry and thirsty land, and has realized that even in those dry places he has in fact been looking for the Lord. Having found nothing in those dry wells, he wisely turns to the place where the Lord may be found—in the sanctuary, the place of worship and meditation. Only the consideration of the beauty and power of the person of Jesus is enough to satisfy the longings of the heart, and those who seek with passion and wisdom will turn their search to where joy may be found.

Prayer: Jesus, my heart is filled with desire, and only You will satisfy my thirsty soul. By Your help I will be wise this day, and seek You where You may be found—in the place of worship and meditative prayer. Let me not be satisfied too easily, but increase the longing in my heart until I seek only You.

Day 2

Psalm 63:3-4

Because Your lovingkindness is better than life, my lips shall praise You. Thus I will bless You while I live; I will lift up my hands in Your name. My soul shall be satisfied as with marrow and fatness, and my mouth shall praise You with joyful lips.

Every individual has the freedom to determine how they are going to spend the resources of their time and energy, and those decisions are based on their perception of what will bring the greatest freedom and fulfillment. The writer here has come to a very important and fundamental understanding: the experiential reality of knowing the love of Christ is more important than any other thing in life. In fact, he has determined that knowing this love is more important than life itself. He would rather forfeit other pleasures and even necessities than miss out on the experience of being loved by God. Therefore, he has set his will to focus on the wisest and most important activity—the worship of God. Anyone who has ever been in love knows about this reality; other things are simply not important. Only the presence and attention of the Beloved is worthy of our full attention, and so we give ourselves to this most important thing—loving God.

Prayer: Oh my Beloved, waken my heart to see the wisdom of loving You as the first thing, the one thing that is necessary. All other realities come into focus when this first thing truly is first. Let Your lovingkindness fill my soul, that I might know life as You intended it to be known.

Day 3

Psalm 63:6-8

When I remember You on my bed, I meditate on You in the night watches. Because You have been my help, therefore in the shadow of Your wings I will rejoice. My soul follows close behind You; Your right hand upholds me.

Who hasn't known those times when sleep is distant and the hours of the night seem far too long? It's often during those sleepless nights that the enemy can come with all his weaponry—worry, anxiety, stress over what needs to be done, and fear that the resources to meet the needs are not going to be in place. In those times he also seems to bring his supply of false comforts, like fantasies and hunger for inadequate stuff, and we find ourselves wanting to eat and drink of the wrong kinds of pleasures.

It seems pretty clear that the writer of this psalm was familiar with those kinds of nights, and yet he found an antidote for the pain. His key? Remember the Lord and meditate upon the beauty of the man Christ Jesus. David's strategy was to let his mind become full of thoughts of the Lord, reviewing the history of God's faithfulness to him, and settling his heart in the comfort of God's constant nature. He sets his soul—mind, will and emotions—squarely in the path of the Holy Spirit, and places himself in God's hand, for only there is he surely secure.

Prayer: Father, I look to You to send Your Spirit to my aid in the night hours, when the enemy's worst seems to plague my soul. You are faithful and kind; Your nature is unchanging, and I will trust in You, following close behind You as You lead me. Thank You, Father!

Day 4

Revelation 21:1-5

Now I saw a new Heaven and a new Earth, for the first Heaven and the first Earth had passed away. Also there was no more sea. Then I, John, saw the holy city, New Jerusalem, coming down out of Heaven from God, prepared as a bride adorned for her husband. And I heard a loud voice from Heaven saying, "Behold, the tabernacle of God is with men, and He will dwell with them, and they shall be His people. God Himself will be with them and be their God. And God will wipe away every tear from their eyes; there shall be no more death, nor sorrow, nor crying. There shall be no more pain, for the former things have passed away." Then He who sat on the throne said, "Behold, I make all things new." And He said to me, "Write, for these words are true and faithful."

I love to read adventure stories and watch movies that are made from books by authors like John Grisham or Tom Clancy. In a well-written story there is always a skillful building of tension, great disasters that loom as not only possible but likely, and surprising twists of deliverance and resolution that leave me cheering that once again the bad guys have been defeated, and the good guys have won. Occasionally, the suspense gets so great that I have to sneak a peek at the ending, just so I can relax.

I think sometimes in the adventure of life, it's good to consider the end of things from time to time for the same reason. God has told us how this adventure called life on Earth is going to end so that we can rest in His marvelous strength and goodness. I encourage you today to consider this passage from Revelation 21 and just let your heart rest in the fact that the outcome of the story is already decided, and not only does the Good Guy win, He gets the girl! Over the next couple of days, we're going to consider this reality, so set your hearts at rest in His sovereign power and might, and give Him thanks that you are included in this great adventure!

Prayer: *Father, thank You that You are the mighty God who sees the end from the beginning, and You have made every provision for the outcome. I give You thanks, Lord, that I am included in this City that is really a Bride, and I can't wait for the story to unfold. Thank You, Lord!*

Day 5

Revelation 21:1-2

Now I saw a new Heaven and a new Earth... Then I, John, saw the holy city, New Jerusalem, coming down out of Heaven from God, prepared as a bride adorned for her Husband.

One of the questions that comes often concerns the focus that we have at the International House of Prayer in Kansas City regarding God's love for His Bride, the Church. We believe that the highest revelation of the identity of His people is that of being the Bride of Christ, and this passage is one of those that helps us understand this. Notice how the apostle John sees the city of God, the New Jerusalem, coming down out of Heaven, but that the city has now been transformed into a glorious Bride! This is an indication that no matter what else we are called as the people of God—His people, His army, His flock, His city, His holy nation, His children, His servants—the culmination of the whole thing is the identity He gives us as the Bride of His beloved Son!

Let your heart focus on this reality for a few moments, and give thanks that no matter where you are in understanding His revelation of your identity, where you are headed is the identity of a Bride perfectly adorned and made beautiful for her Husband. In other words (for you guys that haven't quite got this Bride thing figured out yet!), at the end of the day you will be perfectly prepared as the eternal partner of the Son of God, and He is filled with gladness at that prospect!

***

Prayer: Jesus, I thank You that Your Holy Spirit is working in my heart even now, preparing me to be like You, to be perfectly conformed to what You desire. Open my heart even more to understand what You have in store for me, that I might know the joy of anticipating that day.

Day 6

Revelation 21:3

And I heard a loud voice from Heaven saying, "Behold, the tabernacle of God is with men, and He will dwell with them, and they shall be His people. God Himself will be with them and be their God."

This little verse is one of the most powerful and significant verses in all of Scripture, for it reveals the eternal purpose of God and declares that this purpose will be fulfilled at the culmination of natural history. This eternal purpose is an astonishing reality—the God of the universe wants to be with human beings forever! The phrase "the tabernacle of God is with men" is not referring to an idea that God has a big building that He is going to inhabit, but rather that in Jesus, God has clothed Himself in humanity as His choice of how He wants to spend eternity!

From before the foundations of the Earth, God the Father, the Son and the Holy Spirit decided together that they wanted to have intimate relationship with human beings, and that the only way this could happen was for the Son of God to take a form that would embrace created people. So, *God became a Man.* His decision was to be a human being *forever* so that He could have intimate relationship with people, including you and me. Focus your prayer time today on giving thanks for this astonishing reality that lifts us to an incredible place of dignity and significance.

Prayer: Oh Lord, my heart is stunned as I consider the reality that You desired to be a human being so that I could come to know You. Open my understanding, Lord, that I might comprehend the things You have in store for me as Your Bride and partner, and that You will be my God, and I will be one of Yours forever!

Day 7

Revelation 21:4-5

"And God will wipe away every tear from their eyes; there shall be no more death, nor sorrow, nor crying. There shall be no more pain, for the former things have passed away." Then He who sat on the throne said, "Behold, I make all things new." And He said to me, "Write, for these words are true and faithful."

There is a reality of wonderful comfort in this short passage, for each individual is able to experience the healing power of the Lord as He ministers to His people at the end of the age. Sometimes we can easily believe that God will be close and intimate to everyone else, but it's more difficult to believe that He will come to us individually in that kind of way. But the language in verse four is very clear—God Himself will wipe away *every* tear! In other words, there will be a personal encounter with the living God in which every sorrow that has touched your heart will be healed by the tender touch of the beloved Lord. Nothing that has to do with death, sorrow or crying from pain will touch you ever again! You will never again know pain of any kind, for the King of Heaven, who is your Bridegroom, is going to heal your heart in a deeply personal way.

The good news for us is that we can begin to experience that touch in a real way now, even if not in its fullness. As you fix your attention on the beauty of Jesus and set your heart to worship Him and to believe His Word to you, the Holy Spirit will come in His own way and timing and set your heart in a place of peace. Ask Him to do this today, and wait patiently for the Lord to come to you.

Prayer: Lord Jesus, I bring before You the hurting places of my heart today. I fix my gaze on Your beauty and love, and I ask that Your Spirit would strengthen my heart to receive Your healing touch in Your perfect timing. And as I wait for You, I will worship You, love You and serve You with everything that is in me. Thank You, Lord.

Day 8

Ephesians 1:3-6

Blessed be the God and Father of our Lord Jesus Christ, who has blessed us with every spiritual blessing in the heavenly places in Christ, just as He chose us in Him before the foundation of the world, that we should be holy and without blame before Him in love, having predestined us to adoption as sons by Jesus Christ to Himself, according to the good pleasure of His will, to the praise of the glory of His grace, by which He has made us accepted in the Beloved.

For the next few days, we want to focus on the process that the Father set in place in order to bring His chosen Bride to the reality of the wedding feast in Revelation 19 and 21. The letter from the apostle Paul to the Ephesians is very helpful in giving us some understanding of this. I would encourage you to consider the thoughts in this passage today, and in the following days we'll look at each of the parts.

Notice that this amazing plan is set in place by the Father of our Lord, Jesus Christ, as he orchestrates human history for the pleasure of His Son. See that He has given us all the resources we need—every spiritual blessing in the heavenly places—in order for us to fulfill His purposes for our lives. Consider that the end result has been established in God's mind and heart from before the beginning of time; therefore, your destiny is secure in His love. Understand that His whole point is to include us in His own family by the acceptable activity of Jesus, so that our hope rests completely in Him.

Keep in mind that, in the heart of God, this whole process of redemption is for the purpose of making the wedding feast a reality for His Son. As you pray today, give thanks that you have been included by the will of God, and that His desire is focused upon you as part of His beloved family.

Prayer: *Father, I ask that today You would strengthen my heart in the knowledge of Your definition of my life, and the purpose for which You have created me and redeemed me. Thank You for making me part of Your family, so that my life will bring pleasure to You forever. I worship You, Father, and give You thanks.*

Day 9

Ephesians 1:3

Blessed be the God and Father of our Lord Jesus Christ, who has blessed us with every spiritual blessing in the heavenly places in Christ...

You are invited to consider an amazing reality today—the God of the universe has granted you a standing in His own heart, to be included as a recipient of *every spiritual blessing in the heavenly places in Christ.* This is the kind of statement that is so grandiose that our minds tend to skim over the top of it. But let the words roll around in your mind right now... *every spiritual blessing in the heavenly places.* Such a phrase requires that we come before the Lord and cry out for help from the Holy Spirit to even begin to conceive of what He was thinking when He gave that phrase to Paul. The very blessings of Heaven are already conferred upon us by our Father, who is the Almighty God.

As you pray today, ask the Lord to help you understand these things. Look at verses 17-19 of Ephesians chapter one, and ask the Father to release to you the Spirit of wisdom and understanding, so that you may be able to comprehend at greater levels the joy and beauty in store for you because of Jesus Christ.

Prayer: *Lord Jesus, You who are the giver of the Holy Spirit, release into my heart today the power to comprehend just a little more the realities that You have made available to me. My heart longs to know the truth of who You say I am, and what my inheritance is because of Your great love for me. I'm grateful, Lord, and I thank You and ask You for more.*

Day 10

Ephesians 1:4

Just as He chose us in Him before the foundation of the world, that we should be holy and without blame before Him in love...

I invite you today to fix your thoughts on this reality: you were chosen by God in Christ before the foundation of the world, to fully meet His desires as one He loves. Let me set the scene for you. The Father, the Son and the Holy Spirit were in an eternal relationship of joy and delight. The Son is forever the perfect fulfillment of all that the Father is, the full expression of the heart, mind, will and emotions of God. Hebrews 1:3 calls Jesus the "exact representation of the divine nature." In other words, He is everything that God is.

As the Father gazed eternally on His Son and enjoyed Him, He beheld *in* Him all those who would come *from* Him; generations of children conceived by God in Christ for His own pleasure. Even as the Father delighted in His Son, so He delighted in these children who were seen and chosen before anything else was even created. He saw you in Christ and was well-pleased, for He is confident in His own ability to bring all things into conformity with His will. He has loved you forever, and your destiny is settled in His love. Consider this and give thanks today, asking the Holy Spirit to open your heart and mind to this amazing truth.

Prayer: Father, the thought that I have existed in Your heart from before creation is staggering to me. Help me to set my mind and heart in agreement with the truth that You know me and love me more than I can imagine, and that You have planned my life for Your own enjoyment. Thank You, Lord.

Day 11

Ephesians 1:5

Having predestined us to adoption as sons by Jesus Christ to Himself, according to the good pleasure of His will.

As you meditate on this verse today, keep in mind where this is going: the end of the story is the wedding feast of the Lamb, and you are the Bride! The amazing plan of God from before creation was to bring created people into the eternal family that is called "the Godhead." He purposed in His own heart that you and I would be included in this family, giving His own Son as the one who would accomplish this task by the sacrifice of His own life.

Here's what I want you to focus on today: this was motivated by the good pleasure of His will. The motivating factor in God's decision to include you is good pleasure, or simply, joy. He chose you because your presence in His family gives Him pleasure and joy. The eternal Father has known from eternity that you would be a perfect partner for His Son, and that as He brought you to Himself, His power and love would provide everything you need to fulfill all His desires for you. Your real Father is God, and He is a good Father. He will accomplish all that is needed to present you as a flawless partner for Jesus on the day of His great gladness—the day we all together become His Bride forever!

Prayer: Oh Lord, my heart is overflowing as I consider the astonishing things that You have for me as part of the Bride of Christ. Please help me understand this, and settle my heart in the wondrous truth of Your affections and purpose for my life. I love You, Lord, and I want to know You more.

Day 12

Ephesians 1:6

To the praise of the glory of His grace, by which He has made us accepted in the Beloved.

Today the focus of our attention is that the ultimate purpose of our existence is for all creation to praise the glory of God's grace. In the book of Esther, there was a point in which the king desired to display the beauty of his wife, Queen Vashti, so that the nobles of the kingdom would see the greatness of the king's glory. The apostle Paul tells the Corinthian Believers that even as a man's wife is his glory, so human beings are the glory of God, or in other words, the ultimate revelation of the beauty of God made visible.

So, God's purpose for you is to make you beautiful, to pour out upon you every blessing from heavenly places, to perfectly father you, to present you to His precious Son, Jesus, so that in the perfect revelation of His beauty in you, His Name will be praised by all creation forever. It's as though the Lord is asking the created order, "Do you want to see how majestic I am, how wonderful My grace is? Look at this!" Then He shows you off as His beloved son or daughter, the perfected partner for the one Son, Jesus Christ.

As you pray today, ask the Holy Spirit to settle your mind and heart in this reality, that God has created you for His pleasure, to perfectly reveal His beauty to all creation.

***

Prayer: Lord, help me to get this truth deep into my heart and mind, that I might enjoy You as You enjoy me. Heal the broken places of my heart, so that I might understand and comprehend Your love, which is beyond measure. Thank You, Lord.

Day 13

Proverbs 8:30-31

Then I was beside Him as a master craftsman; and I was daily His delight, rejoicing always before Him, rejoicing in His inhabited world, and My delight was with the sons of men.

These two little verses are the climax of a section of poetic Scripture that speaks about the emotions in the heart of the Godhead as They made the worlds ready for the introduction of human beings onto the scene. Today we want to focus on the delightful, joyous relationship between the Father and the Son as They made preparations for the creation of people for Their own pleasure.

The Person speaking in this passage is identified as "Wisdom," but it becomes clear that the speaker is really the second Person of the Trinity, namely, the Son who would come to Earth as Jesus Christ. He was the "master craftsman," the designer of the creation, and the text says that He was daily the delight of God. The Father's full pleasure is in the Son; everything about Him pleases the Father, for He is the exact image of the divine nature (see Hebrews 1:3).

The Son is pictured as "rejoicing always" in the Father's presence; this is a delightful term that is best translated "to be at play." The creation of the universe, in preparation for the creation of human beings, was the product of a delighted Father and a playful Son who had a wonderful plan for Their own enjoyment. Let your heart consider the reality of an eternally glad God whose pleasure is fully focused on His Son, and on Their mutual plan of having an eternal relationship with you and me!

Prayer: *Holy Spirit, I ask You to reveal the Father's heart to me today. Grant me just a small sense of the Father's pleasure in His Son, and in the work They have done together to create a people for Themselves. I long to know the joy that burns in God's heart, and so I ask for Your help. Thank You.*

Day 14

Proverbs 8:30-31

Then I was beside Him as a master craftsman; and I was daily His delight, rejoicing always before Him, rejoicing in His inhabited world, and My delight was with the sons of men.

Today I want to draw your attention to what was exploding in the heart of Jesus during the process of creating the human race. The Son knew the incredible pleasure of being the Father's delight, and His response was to play in the Father's presence. This is a wonderful insight into the nature of work; God has established work as the creative expression of a playful heart between the Father and the Son.

The Son was rejoicing before the Father; He was spinning, laughing, dancing and creating. Verse 31 tells us that the focus of His rejoicing was the people that inhabited the newly-created world. The next phrase makes it even more clear—*His delight was with the sons of men!* This is a marvelous statement because we get an insight into the very emotions of Jesus as He looks at you and me, awaiting the time when by His own power we will be made ready for Him as the perfect bridal partner.

As you pray today, ask the Holy Spirit to reveal to your heart the truth of how the Lord feels about you. Jesus had no false illusions about your life; He understood that it was going to cost Him His life to have us with Him, and the Scripture says that "for the joy set before Him" He gladly paid the price. You were worth it to Him, and as He considered your life, He was filled with joy from the very beginning of time.

Prayer: *Lord, my heart needs to know this at very basic levels. As I meditate on these truths today, cause me to understand and to come to a place of experiential belief that what You say is true. It's too good not to be true, and I want to know more! Thank You, Lord!*

Day 15

Ephesians 1:17-18

[I pray] that the God of our Lord Jesus Christ, the Father of glory, may give to you the spirit of wisdom and revelation in the knowledge of Him, the eyes of your understanding being enlightened; that you may know what is the hope of His calling, what are the riches of the glory of His inheritance in the saints.

In this passage, the apostle Paul is seeking the release of the Holy Spirit's power on all Believers so that they might know the fullness of God's plan for their lives. Notice the name that he gives to God, *"the Father of glory."* One of the main definitions of glory in the Scripture is the revealed beauty of God, made visible so that people might enjoy and worship Him. Our Father, who planned this whole thing from the beginning, is the Father of all beauty, and He desires to send to us the Spirit of wisdom and revelation so that we might know Him better.

Our hearts have a desperate need to know the Lord better, to understand the kind of God He is, to know His goodness and kindness to us, and that His eternal purpose is for our blessing and fulfillment as the beloved Bride of His Son. In order for this to happen, the ministry of the Holy Spirit is required in our lives. Pray this prayer over your own heart today, that the Father would release the Spirit of wisdom and revelation to you, so that you might come to know God as He really is.

Prayer: Father, send this Spirit of wisdom and revelation to me today. My heart longs to know You more, to see more clearly the kind of God You are, and how You love me. Awaken my heart to Your truth and to the desire that You have for me to understand Your love. Thank You, Lord.

Day 16

Ephesians 1:17-18

[I pray] that the God of our Lord Jesus Christ, the Father of glory, may give to you the spirit of wisdom and revelation in the knowledge of Him, the eyes of your understanding being enlightened; that you may know what is the hope of His calling, what are the riches of the glory of His inheritance in the saints.

Paul's prayer has three points of focus that are revealed in verse 18: that our understanding would be awakened, that we might know the hope of our calling, and that we might comprehend the rich glory of God's inheritance in us.

There is a longing in our hearts to be awakened to the knowledge and understanding of the nature, character and purposes of God. In our human weakness, we do not have the ability to comprehend these realities, and so in a miraculous way, God has provided the one and only door for understanding. His Holy Spirit will come to our human spirits and awaken the knowledge of eternal things. All He asks is that we acknowledge our need for this, saying, "Lord, I admit that in my own strength I am blind and confused. But You will send help to me, Lord, by the power of Your Spirit. Touch my eyes, Lord; I want to see."

This prayer of humility is pleasing to the Lord, and He is delighted to release to us the power to see and know Him as He really is. Make this your prayer today.

———

Prayer: Lord, I so desperately need and want to know who You are, and how You feel and think concerning me. I know I can't understand this without Your Spirit revealing it to me, and so I ask for what You have promised. Thank You, Lord.

Day 17

Ephesians 1:17-18

[I pray] that the God of our Lord Jesus Christ, the Father of glory, may give to you the spirit of wisdom and revelation in the knowledge of Him, the eyes of your understanding being enlightened; that you may know what is the hope of His calling, what are the riches of the glory of His inheritance in the saints.

I want to draw your focus today to the knowledge of the hope of His calling. Remember, the whole point of the creation of human beings is for the pleasure of God in relationship with us, and in order for that to happen we must come into His likeness and character. In Paul's letter to the Colossian Believers, he makes a marvelous statement that settles in us the issue of hope that God's purposes will in fact be accomplished. He reminds the readers that the Holy Spirit has revealed the "glorious mystery" of God's plan, namely, "Christ [is] in you, the hope of glory (Colossians 1:27)."

This little sentence is packed with power, for we are being told that Jesus Christ Himself has come to live within our hearts by the Holy Spirit, and therefore the completion of His purpose is a certain thing. Redemption is far more than just being rescued from Hell; it is the release into our hearts of the power of God to accomplish His will and destiny for us.

Today let your heart be filled with the good truth that Jesus lives within you and is working night and day to make you a suitable partner for Himself. He will accomplish it, for you are all that He desires!

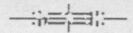

Prayer: *Lord, my heart is stunned that You would come and live in me by Your Spirit, that You would ensure by Your own power the fulfillment of my destiny as Your partner. The thought is more than I can bear, but I ask You again to help me get it! I love You, Lord, and my heart aches to be a worthy partner of this Man, Christ Jesus.*

Day 18

Ephesians 1:17-18

[I pray] that the God of our Lord Jesus Christ, the Father of glory, may give to you the spirit of wisdom and revelation in the knowledge of Him, the eyes of your understanding being enlightened; that you may know what is the hope of His calling, what are the riches of the glory of His inheritance in the saints.

One final glance at this passage, focusing today on the very last phrase, "what are the riches of the glory of His inheritance in the saints." This is a segment that is filled with wonder, and is worthy of much meditation and prayerful consideration. Several thoughts: first, it is a staggering thought that God would have an inheritance in human beings. We usually consider an inheritance as something that comes from beyond us, that makes us more wealthy, or gives us something that makes our lives more enjoyable. And the truth of this phrase is that God, the Creator of all things, has decided that an eternal relationship with you and me is going to make His perfect existence even better! What a mind-boggling idea! Toss that one around in your mind and heart for a few thousand years and see what happens!

Secondly, let's consider what this inheritance is to Him. Remember, the whole point of creating us was to have intimate relationship with Himself, namely as the Bride of His Son Jesus. In Genesis 1:18, God speaks to Adam as the first man, and promises him a "helper comparable" to him. We know from Ephesians five that the Genesis passage is a picture of Christ and the Church, so what God is setting in place here is a picture of what we are to Him—a helper comparable to His Son, the perfect counterpart, the partner in ministry that will walk alongside the Son as co-heirs of the Kingdom of God. Let your heart be expanded with the truth of this, asking the Holy Spirit to empower you to receive and understand what He has in mind as His glorious inheritance in the saints.

$$\cdot\rlap{\,}{\rule{0pt}{0pt}}\text{---}\rlap{\,}{\rule{0pt}{0pt}}$$

Prayer: *Jesus, my little mind is too small to comprehend the reality of this, beyond just saying the words. Send Your Spirit to open my understanding, so that I may know Your thoughts and sense the joy of Your heart as You look forward to my becoming all You have created me to be.*

Day 19

Ephesians 3:14-19

For this reason I bow my knees to the Father of our Lord Jesus Christ, from whom the whole family in Heaven and Earth is named, that He would grant you, according to the riches of His glory, to be strengthened with might through His Spirit in the inner man, that Christ may dwell in your hearts through faith; that you, being rooted and grounded in love, may be able to comprehend with all the saints what is the width and length and depth and height—to know the love of Christ which passes knowledge; that you may be filled with all the fullness of God.

As we consider this passage over the next few days, there are several points of focus that I will draw to your attention. There is a wonderful and natural progression of revelation that is put forward here, beginning with the loving Father who sends His Spirit for the purpose of strengthening our hearts. The reason that our hearts need strength is to empower us to receive the presence of Jesus inside, establishing us in the love of the Father. In the context of this seedbed of unconditional love, we grow up into the ability to know the full love of Christ, a love that is incomprehensible apart from the power of God.

The end result of this process is beyond imagination—the knowledge of the love of Christ that fills us with all the fullness of God. This is an unbelievable statement, one of those things that, were it not in the Bible, would sound like heresy. The fact is that God has some things in store for us that will boggle our minds. Fix your heart on these things and ask the Holy Spirit to prepare you to consider them over the next few days.

Prayer: *Jesus, my heart is overwhelmed at who You are and who You say that I am. Send me Your Holy Spirit and open my heart to understanding, for I deeply desire to know the things You have for me, together with all the saints. Thank You, Jesus.*

Day 20

Ephesians 3:14-19

For this reason I bow my knees to the Father of our Lord Jesus Christ, from whom the whole family in Heaven and Earth is named, that He would grant you, according to the riches of His glory, to be strengthened with might through His Spirit in the inner man, that Christ may dwell in your hearts through faith; that you, being rooted and grounded in love, may be able to comprehend with all the saints what is the width and length and depth and height—to know the love of Christ which passes knowledge; that you may be filled with all the fullness of God.

Paul begins here with an appeal to the Father of the Lord Jesus Christ, who is the source of all fatherhood in Heaven and on Earth. This is a power-packed phrase, because it settles for us the reality that our true Father is God Himself, and that we were not brought forth out of mere human process or desire, but by the will of God. In understanding this, we echo what John states in his gospel that we are those "who were born, not of blood, nor of the will of the flesh, nor of the will of man, but of God (John 1:13)."

This is a most important understanding for us to focus on in prayer. You exist because of the desire of God, not because there was a human interaction between a man and a woman. *Regardless of your life history, whether you have had the most horrible or the most wonderful background, the reason you are alive is because God desired you and has caused you to come into relationship with Him for His express pleasure and purpose.* Ask the Holy Spirit to open your understanding to this reality, that He desires and loves you in the perfection of His fatherly heart.

Prayer: *Father of glory, send Your Spirit to me today and help me. I long to know the kind of love that You have for me, a love that is beyond my comprehension without the help of Your Spirit. Thank You for loving me more than I can understand, and strengthen me to understand. Thank You, Lord.*

Day 21

Ephesians 3:14-19

For this reason I bow my knees to the Father of our Lord Jesus Christ, from whom the whole family in Heaven and Earth is named, that He would grant you, according to the riches of His glory, to be strengthened with might through His Spirit in the inner man, that Christ may dwell in your hearts through faith; that you, being rooted and grounded in love, may be able to comprehend with all the saints what is the width and length and depth and height—to know the love of Christ which passes knowledge; that you may be filled with all the fullness of God.

The first focal point of Paul's prayer for the Ephesians is found in verse 16, namely that God Himself would grant each person the strengthening power of His Spirit so we can realize His purposes in our lives. A couple of ideas for your consideration: first, remember that it is the Holy Spirit inspiring Paul to pray this prayer over Christians. God has designed reality so that His power is loosed upon the Earth through human beings who agree with His character and His purposes on the Earth. It is the will of God to empower you to believe and receive His love, and His way is to find human intercessors (us) who will agree with His agenda so that He can release this power to mankind.

Isaiah 59 tells us that God Himself provided this intercessor (Jesus, of course!) when He couldn't find another willing human, and now Paul is standing in that role. The Father's purpose is to give you His very strength, the Spirit of the Father, to empower you to receive His love and believe what He has in store for you. Bring your heart and mind into agreement with that today, concerning your own life and the lives of those you love, and ask for the Spirit of the Father to be released with power into your heart.

Prayer: *Father of glory, I agree with You that Your purpose is to reveal Your love to my weak heart. Send Your Spirit today; establish me in the truth of who You are and of who You say that I am. Thank You for loving me, and for helping me to know Your love in the deep places of my heart.*

Day 22

Ephesians 3:14-19

For this reason I bow my knees to the Father of our Lord Jesus Christ, from whom the whole family in Heaven and Earth is named, that He would grant you, according to the riches of His glory, to be strengthened with might through His Spirit in the inner man, that Christ may dwell in your hearts through faith; that you, being rooted and grounded in love, may be able to comprehend with all the saints what is the width and length and depth and height—to know the love of Christ which passes knowledge; that you may be filled with all the fullness of God.

There is a powerful reality communicated in these verses that can be understood when we remember that God's whole point in creating human beings was to present us as the Bride of Christ, the perfect counterpart to His Son, Jesus. In Ephesians 3:17-19, we are shown an incredible plan for the perfecting process given to us by the mercy of God. By the ministry of the Spirit of the Father, Christ Himself takes up residence in our hearts by faith, and His initial role is to establish a groundwork of confidence in the Father's love. Like a flowerbed prepared with good soil, nutrients and water, the heart of the Believer is prepared to receive the seeds of God's love as our Father, so that we may grow up with the capacity to receive the love of Jesus as our Bridegroom. A bride must be well-fathered before she can be well-married, and this passage shows us how God intends to prepare us for this.

As you pray today, ask the Holy Spirit to ground you in the knowledge of the Father's love, so that the revelation of the love of Jesus as your Bridegroom can be released to you in the perfect timing of your heavenly Father.

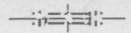

Prayer: *Jesus, I long to be established and unshakable in the knowledge of the Father's love just as You are. I believe this is what You want for me, so today I agree with You and ask that as I read Your Word, sing Your songs and talk with You, the roots of Your love will go deep.*

Day 23

Ephesians 3:14-19

For this reason I bow my knees to the Father of our Lord Jesus Christ, from whom the whole family in Heaven and Earth is named, that He would grant you, according to the riches of His glory, to be strengthened with might through His Spirit in the inner man, that Christ may dwell in your hearts through faith; that you, being rooted and grounded in love, may be able to comprehend with all the saints what is the width and length and depth and height—to know the love of Christ which passes knowledge; that you may be filled with all the fullness of God.

Here is the point of the whole process of being established in the love of the Father—*to know the love of Jesus, which is beyond comprehension, and to be filled with all the fullness of God.* This is an astonishing verse, one that would be impossible to believe if it were not in Scripture. Paul gets so caught up in his excitement over the love of Christ being revealed that before he realizes it, he's talking about four dimensions of Christ's love! It's incomprehensible, and yet God intends to reveal it to us by the power of His own Spirit!

We might ask how a human can be filled with all the fullness of God. I don't know the answer, but I do know that it has already happened once—in the person of Jesus Christ. He was a man completely filled with the presence and power of God. And because He lived as a man in that way, so too will you and I as we are conformed to His image and identity as His Bride. As you meditate on this overwhelming truth today, give thanks and ask the Lord of glory to reveal these things to your heart.

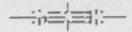

Prayer: *Jesus, just the thought of these things makes my head spin with wonder and delight. Could it be that You really love me like this, and that You will show me the fullness of Your own identity as the Lord of the universe? Oh, my God, increase my faith! Thank You for loving me.*

Day 24

Ephesians 5:25-32

Husbands, love your wives, just as Christ also loved the Church and gave Himself for her, that He might sanctify and cleanse her with the washing of water by the word, that He might present her to Himself a glorious Church, not having spot or wrinkle or any such thing, but that she should be holy and without blemish. So husbands ought to love their own wives as their own bodies; he who loves his wife loves himself. For no one ever hated his own flesh, but nourishes and cherishes it, just as the Lord does the Church. For we are members of His Body, of His flesh and of His bones. "For this reason a man shall leave his father and mother and be joined to his wife, and the two shall become one flesh." This is a great mystery, but I speak concerning Christ and the Church.

This passage has long been seen as one of the primary passages about marriage, and is often used as a basis of exhortation at weddings and occasions of similar emphasis. What seems increasingly clear, however, is that far too little energy has been expended coming to a place of experiential understanding of the romantic love of Jesus for the Church, which is the real focus of the passage.

Consider the statements made concerning the purpose of Jesus' self-sacrifice on behalf of His Bride: He loved her, He gave Himself for her, to wash and cleanse her, to present her to Himself as glorious, fully perfect and without fault. He loves us as He loves Himself, and He nourishes and cherishes us with the singular goal of becoming one flesh! What a mystery!

Over the next several days, we're going to focus on specific phrases in this passage, but today let your prayer be one of preparation, that the Holy Spirit will make your heart ready to receive these things.

Prayer: Jesus, this is such a familiar passage, but I ask You today to give me a new ability to comprehend what is being said here, and to experience what it is to be loved by You in this way. I long to know this love, Lord! Help me, for Your own sake.

Day 25

Ephesians 5:25-32

Husbands, love your wives, just as Christ also loved the Church and gave Himself for her, that He might sanctify and cleanse her with the washing of water by the word, that He might present her to Himself a glorious Church, not having spot or wrinkle or any such thing, but that she should be holy and without blemish. So husbands ought to love their own wives as their own bodies; he who loves his wife loves himself. For no one ever hated his own flesh, but nourishes and cherishes it, just as the Lord does the Church. For we are members of His Body, of His flesh and of His bones. "For this reason a man shall leave his father and mother and be joined to his wife, and the two shall become one flesh." This is a great mystery, but I speak concerning Christ and the Church.

Our focus today is on the cleansing and sanctifying properties of the Word of God that prepare us for being presented to Jesus as His Bride on that day. In the second chapter of the book of Esther, we are told how Esther, as one of the candidates to become the Queen of King Xerxes, was taken through a 12-month process of baths and perfume applications so that she would be ready for the day of her presentation to the king. When that day came, she was radiant and totally pleasing to him, and was declared to be the king's new bride!

This is what happens to us when we take the Word of God into our hearts on a frequent and consistent basis through meditation and through devotional prayer. The Spirit of Jesus uses the Word to cleanse and prepare us in the beauty of holiness so that we will be like Him on that day. Notice how our interaction with the Word is not to be a dutiful thing, but something that is driven by romance and by the anticipation of His great pleasure in us. As you meditate on the Word today and in the coming days, let your heart be settled in the truth of His love, and that you are being made ready to meet Him on that day!

Prayer: *Jesus, come wash me with Your Word! Make me ready for Your own pleasure, and cause me to desire the preparations that You have set in place with me in mind. Thank You for loving me enough to prepare me for Your good pleasure.*

Day 26

Ephesians 5:25-32

Husbands, love your wives, just as Christ also loved the Church and gave Himself for her, that He might sanctify and cleanse her with the washing of water by the word, that He might present her to Himself a glorious Church, not having spot or wrinkle or any such thing, but that she should be holy and without blemish. So husbands ought to love their own wives as their own bodies; he who loves his wife loves himself. For no one ever hated his own flesh, but nourishes and cherishes it, just as the Lord does the Church. For we are members of His Body, of His flesh and of His bones. "For this reason a man shall leave his father and mother and be joined to his wife, and the two shall become one flesh." This is a great mystery, but I speak concerning Christ and the Church.

In verse 27 we are given a clear insight into the ultimate purpose that Jesus has in His mind for you as part of His corporate Bride. The entire goal of His plan of salvation, indeed of the whole history of His interaction with human beings, is to have a Bride made ready to present to Himself on that day. The text says that He will present to Himself a "glorious Church" without any fault, or blemish, or wrinkle—in other words, flawless even as He is flawless!

The term "glory" is used in the Bible to speak of the revealed beauty of God, the manifestation of His ultimate beauty that is called the "holiness of God." The Spirit of God is going to make you and me beautiful, that is, fully conformed to His character and nature, perfectly finished as the suitable partner for His incomparable Son. All of the Father's energy throughout history has been focused on this reality, and everything He has done in relationship with His people as a whole, and with us as individuals, is to get us ready for that day.

This past June I had the privilege of performing the wedding ceremony for my son and his bride. As I stood on the platform watching the bridesmaids enter, I wondered what the Lord was going to speak to my heart in the following moments. When Stephanie entered the sanctuary on the arm of her father, the power of the Holy Spirit hit my heart, and I heard the Lord speak to my heart, "Behold the glory of a Bride made ready for a Son who is worthy!" My heart was stunned by this statement, and by the realization that this is my destiny, along with all those who claim His name as their own.

Prayer: Jesus, open my heart to this amazing truth, that You are going to make me beautiful for Your own pleasure, and on that day, together with all the saints, I will be just what You desire. I long to comprehend this more and more. Instruct my heart, oh Lord, that I might wait with joy for the revelation of Your love.

Day 27

Ephesians 5:25-32

Husbands, love your wives, just as Christ also loved the Church and gave Himself for her, that He might sanctify and cleanse her with the washing of water by the word, that He might present her to Himself a glorious Church, not having spot or wrinkle or any such thing, but that she should be holy and without blemish. So husbands ought to love their own wives as their own bodies; he who loves his wife loves himself. For no one ever hated his own flesh, but nourishes and cherishes it, just as the Lord does the Church. For we are members of His Body, of His flesh and of His bones. "For this reason a man shall leave his father and mother and be joined to his wife, and the two shall become one flesh." This is a great mystery, but I speak concerning Christ and the Church.

It is essential as we consider this matter of being fully pleasing to the Lord that we understand it is the power of His Word that accomplishes this in our lives. It is the Lord who is the one at work here, the one who does the sanctifying and cleansing work through the speaking of His Word to our hearts. The only thing that is required of us is that we come before Him with an open heart so that we might receive the word that is spoken over us.

The quickest way to accomplish this is to take the Word of God, the Bible, and find the passages that speak of His faithfulness, His goodness, His holiness and love, and pray those passages over our own hearts in a devotional way. Doing this in a context of worship and of occasional fasting from food speeds up the process by opening our spirit to His presence and work. The best passages include the Psalms and the "Apostolic Prayers" of the New Testament[1]. As you do this, set your heart and mind in agreement with what God says about Himself and about you. As the Word of God enters your spirit, you are cleansed from the inside out as the power of the Word has its effect. Establishing a regular pattern of devotional prayer straight from the Word of God is the quickest way to experience the joy of His sanctifying work in your heart.

Prayer: *Jesus, come to me and do Your work of preparation, for I desire nothing more than to be made ready for You when You return for me. I long to be like You, and I believe that You love me enough to do what is necessary in my life. Thank You, Lord!*

---

[1] To view IHOP's downloadable documents, including the Apostolic Prayers in PDF format, please go to http://www.fotb.com/ihopkc/IHOP_downloads.asp.

Day 28

Ephesians 5:25-32

Husbands, love your wives, just as Christ also loved the Church and gave Himself for her, that He might sanctify and cleanse her with the washing of water by the word, that He might present her to Himself a glorious Church, not having spot or wrinkle or any such thing, but that she should be holy and without blemish. So husbands ought to love their own wives as their own bodies; he who loves his wife loves himself. For no one ever hated his own flesh, but nourishes and cherishes it, just as the Lord does the Church. For we are members of His Body, of His flesh and of His bones. "For this reason a man shall leave his father and mother and be joined to his wife, and the two shall become one flesh." This is a great mystery, but I speak concerning Christ and the Church.

Verse 29 of Ephesians five tells us that Jesus loves the Church just like He loves His own flesh, and because of that love, He is focused on nurturing and cherishing His Body, which is His Bride. This truth touches a very deep place in our hearts, because inside every one of us burns this longing to be loved in an ultimate and perfect way. There is something inside that tells us that we should be the focus of someone's perfect love. We were made to be cherished and nourished by someone whose love is perfect and never-ending.

The good news is that we have a Bridegroom whose love is like that! God has decided that it is in His best interest to love us as He loves Himself, and because He is worthy of perfect love, His love for Himself is flawless and perfect. So, because God can only love in a perfect way, His love for you is that same kind of love. Jesus prayed in John 17:23 that we would come to know that the Father loves us even as He loves the Son. That is a staggering prayer, and one that is worthy of our meditation. I am loved by the Father in the same way that He loves the Son, and loved by the Son with that same perfect love; I will certainly be made ready for my eternal destiny as His partner, His Bride. Fix your thoughts on these things day by day, regardless of circumstances or feelings, and watch the Holy Spirit change you from the inside out!

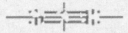

Prayer: Lord, Your Word is so amazing to me, and it causes me to face the fact that You have made provision for every one of my desires. Help me comprehend Your love; open my heart and mind to know and to understand, and to love You in return for what You have done. Thank You, Lord.

Day 29

Ephesians 5:25-32

Husbands, love your wives, just as Christ also loved the Church and gave Himself for her, that He might sanctify and cleanse her with the washing of water by the word, that He might present her to Himself a glorious Church, not having spot or wrinkle or any such thing, but that she should be holy and without blemish. So husbands ought to love their own wives as their own bodies; he who loves his wife loves himself. For no one ever hated his own flesh, but nourishes and cherishes it, just as the Lord does the Church. For we are members of His body, of His flesh and of His bones. "For this reason a man shall leave his father and mother and be joined to his wife, and the two shall become one flesh." This is a great mystery, but I speak concerning Christ and the Church.

One final thought from this amazing passage. Verse 31 informs us that the standard of marriage is that a man leaves his father and mother to be joined to his wife, and the two of them become one flesh. This idea is first presented way back at the beginning of creation when God speaks it to Adam in Genesis 2:24. Most people assume that God is instructing Adam about what his commitment should be like, but God is not speaking to Adam about himself. This becomes clear when we realize that Adam didn't leave anyone; he had no mother and father to leave! God made him out of the dust, and so that phrase could not be applicable to him in a primary way.

The fact is, God the Father was already giving us an insight into His own commitment to send His Son Jesus to become a human being. Jesus is the one who would leave the Father's home and cling to His Bride by becoming one flesh with her. The fact that the Son of God became a human being forever is the ultimate expression of this commitment, and it is an astonishing affirmation of His determination to love us forever. The reason He is so committed to our perfection and fulfillment is that He can't go back! He is a man *forever*, and will for His own sake finish the work He has begun with you and me.

Set your heart and mind on these things, and meditate on God's eternal commitment to you as the Bride of His precious Son.

Prayer: *Oh Lord, You have given me just the smallest understanding of these things, and yet my heart is full to overflowing at the enormity of Your love for me! It is astounding that You would become a human being, with all of the implications of opening Your heart to weakness and pain, simply for the love of Your Bride! Help me see, oh Lord, that I may be strengthened in Your love this day. Thank You.*

Day 30

Numbers 6:22-27

And the Lord spoke to Moses, saying: "Speak to Aaron and his sons, saying, 'This is the way you shall bless the children of Israel.' Say to them: 'The Lord bless you and keep you; the Lord make His face shine upon you, and be gracious to you; the Lord lift up His countenance upon you, and give you peace.' So they shall put My name on the children of Israel, and I will bless them."

I want to finish this 31-day devotional guide with two meditations on one of the great passages of blessing in Scripture. The priestly blessing of Numbers six is such a wonderful window into the heart of the Father as He prepares His people to be the Bride of His Son, and my prayer is that you will make a habit of meditating on this blessing, and of speaking it over your own life frequently, if not daily.

The blessing itself, found in verses 24-26, helps us to know that one of the basic longings of a child's heart is satisfied by the Father, which is the longing to be seen and noticed by Him. The power of this verse is in the knowledge that God has set His eyes upon you, and that His gaze is not the disapproving glare of an angry parent, but the tender, gracious and peace-imparting gaze of a Father of infinite love. His gaze gives to us the place of approval, of delight and of peace.

When my children were small, one of their constant requests was, "Daddy, watch me!" It's a longing in every child's heart to be noticed, approved and loved in such a way that it is communicated through the loving gaze of the Father's eyes. The greatest blessing we can have is to know that the God of the universe is our Father, and that He looks upon us every day with delight, joy, approval and grace. I pray that you are strengthened in this knowledge today.

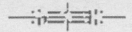

Prayer: *Oh Father, thank You that Your eyes are fixed upon me, and that in Your gaze is my life. Thank You that You see me and that You notice my feeble attempts to please You, even if I'm clumsy or foolish in my immaturity. I love You, Lord, and long to live in the pleasure of Your gaze forever.*

Day 31

Numbers 6:22-27

And the Lord spoke to Moses, saying: "Speak to Aaron and his sons, saying, 'This is the way you shall bless the children of Israel.' Say to them: 'The Lord bless you and keep you; the Lord make His face shine upon you, and be gracious to you; the Lord lift up His countenance upon you, and give you peace.' So they shall put My name on the children of Israel, and I will bless them."

One final focus: the reason that God gave this blessing to the priests to speak over the people is found in verse 27. "So they shall put My name on the children of Israel, and I will bless them." What I want to point out that is so powerful here is the language of covenant relationships. God's desire is that His name would be put upon His children! This is marriage language, the language of permanence and inclusion, and it awakens us to the fact that God has always desired that we become part of His family.

I love how the apostle Peter speaks of this in his first letter, chapter two, verse ten: "...[you] who once were not a people, but are now the people of God..." In our natural state, before we received the grace of God through the initiative of the Holy Spirit, we were "not a people"; in other words, we had no identity, no name. But now, God has given us His name, He has included us in His family, and we are now the people of blessing, the recipients of God's covenant of mercy and blessing.

God has set His heart to bless you. You are loved beyond your capacity to comprehend it. My prayer for you is that you would fix your eyes upon Him, and invite the Holy Spirit to teach you and lead you into the wonderful knowledge of the love of Christ for you as His Bride.

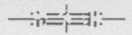

Prayer: *Thank You for loving me, Lord. My heart is stirred with longing and wonder as I meditate on Your love. Send Your Holy Spirit to me that I may know more and more of Your love. And Lord, please come quickly, for I long to be with You forever. Amen.*

CHAPTER VI

Secrets of the Secret Place

Bob Sorge

Formerly the Director of Music at Elim Bible Institute, a Bible school instructor, assistant pastor, and senior pastor, Bob Sorge shares from experience that is deeply rooted in personal intimacy with Jesus. He travels through the valley of a sustained physical trial while holding to the contagious hope God has given him for a mighty deliverance. Bob currently bases his international traveling and writing ministry from Kansas City, Missouri. His wife, Marci, serves on the leadership team of the International House of Prayer in Kansas City, and their children, Joel, Katie and Michael, are actively involved with them in the ministry of IHOP-KC.

The devotionals from this month are excerpted and abridged from Bob's book, Secrets of the Secret Place, which is an overflow of his life of prayer. Bob's other books include: Pain, Perplexity and Promotion (an interpretation of the book of Job); Dealing with the Praise and Rejection of Man; Envy: The Enemy Within; Exploring Worship; In His Face; The Fire of Delayed Answers; The Fire of God's Love; Following the River: A Vision for Corporate Worship; Loyalty: the Reach of the Noble Heart, and one more book to be released in 2004. To empower and inspire your secret relationship with God, study guides are available for several of his books. For more information on Bob's traveling and writing ministry, we invite you to visit his website at www.oasishouse.net.

Day 1 – The Secret of Listening

John 10:27

My sheep hear My voice, and I know them, and they follow Me.

God has always designed that the secret place be a place where He answers us and speaks to us.

Sometimes, He even apprehends us by thundering to us with His awesome voice. There is nothing more glorious in all of life than hearing His voice! God has always longed to have the kind of intimate relationship with His people wherein they hear His voice and respond accordingly.

We close the door to our secret place so that we might shut out all distracting voices and tune our hearts to the one voice which we long to hear. It's a great delight to talk to God, but it's even more thrilling when He talks to us. I've discovered that He has more important things to say than I do. Things don't change when I talk to God; things change when God talks to me. When I talk, nothing happens; when God talks, the universe comes into existence. So the power of prayer is found, not in convincing God of my agenda, but in waiting upon Him to hear His agenda. My role in the secret place is to listen for anything God might want to speak. If He doesn't speak to me, my time spent in silent listening is not futile or vain. I haven't missed something or failed to connect. I've done my part. I realize I can't tell God what to speak, or when to speak it. But I can position myself in the secret place so that, when He chooses to speak, I am found listening.

Hearing God is the most cherished secret of the secret place. You *can* hear the voice of God. Stop everything, come aside, listen and wait on Him. Wait until. He longs to commune with you.

Be encouraged by the fact that you're not the only one who finds listening a very challenging discipline to master. The best attainments in God always come the hardest. Be prepared to make the discipline of attentive listening a lifetime pursuit that will become easier in the doing it.

Prayer: *Lord, You created the universe with a word. Hearing Your voice is the wellspring of eternal life; it is the fountainhead of Kingdom power and authority; it is the source of wisdom, understanding and life direction! Nothing can replace the confidence and authority that come from hearing You. May hearing Your voice become the singular quest of my heart, the sole pursuit that alone satisfies the great longings of my heart! Speak to me, Father. I long to listen!*

Day 2 – The Secret of Burning

Proverbs 6:27-28

Can a man take fire to his bosom and his clothes not be burned? Can one walk on hot coals, and his feet not be seared?

When you draw close to the fire of God's Word, you are actually taking fire into your bosom—and the leprous, filthy clothes of your old life are being burned away. Your feet are being seared to walk in the way of holiness and righteousness and obedience. It's impossible to embrace this living fire and not be changed!

It's the secret place that lights our fire, that sets us burning. I'm talking about white-hot, fiery zeal for the face of Jesus and for the concerns of His Kingdom. Jesus came to kindle a fire on Earth (Luke 12:49) by which He intended to set us ablaze with His very own passions and desires. To maintain its intensity, this fire must be constantly stoked by the intimate passions of the secret place.

You are destined for fire. You will burn for all eternity—the only question is *where*. Your greatest desire is to be a living flame, ignited with the exhilaration of beholding His beauty, worshiping Him with uninhibited abandon and deployed into the world with self-controlled, calculated zeal that does not love its own life even unto death.

God's Word is a fire, and His presence is totally engulfed in fire. When you approach God, you are drawing near to the great blazing inferno of the ages. To be set on fire, you must get close to God.

Do you desire a greater compulsion for the secret place? Invite the Burning One, the Holy Spirit, to ignite the eternal flame of His fiery jealousy in your life. The Scripture says, "The Spirit who dwells in us yearns jealously

(James 4:5)." The agenda of this yearning jealousy is that Christ's Bride might be set ablaze with an exclusive and fiery passion for her Beloved.

Prayer: Holy Spirit, let your burning jealousy have its consuming way in my life, until every competing affection and false god is completely burned away and until one raging, all-consuming passion fills my entire being—love for the altogether Lovely One, the Man Christ Jesus.

Day 3 – The Secret of Violence

Matthew 11:12

The Kingdom of Heaven suffers violence, and the violent take it by force.

Genuine faith seeks God earnestly. True faith understands not only that God exists, but that He rewards us according to the intensity of our pursuit of Him.

Spiritual violence begins in the secret place. It all starts with how you apply yourself to the disciplines of prayer—adoration, gazing, fasting, reading, study, meditation, listening, absorption of truth. This is where violence starts. One of the most violent things you'll ever do is wrestle down all the competing elements in your calendar and consistently carve out the time to shut yourself into the secret place. The person of violence and wisdom will enact whatever measures are necessary to be alert and engaged on a regular basis in this, the most delightful portion of the day. To gain this treasure, you must go mining fiercely for it (Proverbs 2:4, 7).

The term "spiritual violence" captures the intensity with which the last days' generation will pursue God. They will seek God with their entire being, denying themselves and throwing off all entangling sins in order to run the race with passion, purity and perseverance.

I get inspired when I read the stories of the great Christian runners of history. I was so stirred in my spirit when I read the story of how Francis of Assisi pursued God in his early twenties. One of his companions tells the story of how Francis crawled out of bed after he thought his companion was asleep. He knelt on the floor, and for the better part of the night prayed one single sentence: "My God and my all." Then he caught a little bit of sleep and awoke with the others. Such an intense pace!

Go after God! No one else can hinder your race. It doesn't matter if other people might not recognize your ministry—pursue God! Choirs of saints are cheering for you from the banisters of Heaven. "We finished the course by God's grace," they're crying, "You can, too!"

Prayer: *Father, I believe You will reward my relentless pursuit of You. Help me to exchange my natural zeal for true spiritual fervency. When no one is looking, I want to be energized by that inward, holy fire that still burns. Cause the first command to be in first place in my life.*

Day 4 – The Secret of Humility

1 Peter 5:6-7

Therefore humble yourselves under the mighty hand of God, that He may exalt you in due time, casting all your care upon Him, for He cares for you.

Our violent pursuit of God must be wedded to a gentle and humble spirit. Humility is the foundation of all prayer. Humility says, "Lord, I am empty without Your fullness; I am broken without Your wholeness; I am helpless without Your strength; I am clueless without Your wisdom. Apart from You I am nothing. I need You! I need You so desperately that I am pouring myself out to You here in the secret place."

We begin to trim back on our secret time with God when we're feeling great about ourselves, energetic and optimistic about our future, and confident about the path we're taking. It's the first sign that were getting full of ourselves.

Once you see His greatness and your bankruptcy, there comes great joy in humbling yourself before the Lord. With what delight the elders cast their crowns at the foot of the throne! They take what represents the aggregate compilation of all their achievements and throw it all down at the feet of Him from whom it all proceeded in the first place. He gave it to us that we might give it all back to Him.

None of this was our idea, it all started with Him and it all ends with Him (Romans 11:36). He dignifies us that we might have something to lay before Him in humility and devotion. God dignifies us—with sonship, glory, acceptance, royalty, purpose, significance, wealth, honor, salvation, wisdom, revelation, understanding, status, character, holiness, victories—so that we might enjoy the highest privilege of casting it all at His feet. Throw yourself at His feet today; He is worthy of the highest praise.

Prayer: *Omniscient Father, search my heart and my motives. Open my eyes to my true state of being, and to Your greatness. Drive me to my knees, back to the source of all wisdom, back to "the eternal, immortal, only wise God." I have made You too small in my eyes; magnify Yourself once again. May I see that all You do is wise, and in humility I will praise You.*

Day 5 – The Secret of Watching

Mark 13:32-33, 37

But of that day and hour no one knows, not even the angels in Heaven, nor the Son, but only the Father. Take heed, watch and pray for you do not know when the time is... And what I say to you, I say to all: Watch!

Jesus connected prayerfulness with vigilant watching. Twice He told His disciples, "Watch and pray (Mark 13:33)." So there's something about prayer that is wide-eyed, attentive and on full mental alert. Sadly, far too many Believers are asleep in this the most momentous hour of human history.

In the secret place, we do not hide from current events like an ostrich burying its head in the sand; rather, we bring our awareness of current events to the searching lamp of the Scriptures and the Spirit of God. The Lord never places on us the burden of seeing into the future; that is His job. He does call us, though, to be alert to the hour in which we live and to discern the signs of our times. He expects us to have understanding and awareness concerning *today*.

One of the most important words of this hour is the word *discernment*. Jesus wants us to be alert and able to discern the signs of the times. Discernment will be cultivated, not by reading the morning newspaper, but by reading God's Word. We gain discernment only through the Holy Spirit (Philippians 1:9). Those who stand at attention in the secret place will carry the wisdom to discern the mystery of iniquity and the mystery of godliness in the Earth today.

There are times in my secret place when I put everything else aside, such as my reading or requests, and just pause to ask this question, "Lord, what are You doing in the Earth today? What themes are You emphasizing right now? Among which groups of people are You moving in an unusual way? What do You want me to see concerning the day and hour in which I live? What is my role in Your present activities?" Then I wait upon Him for insight and understanding.

Oh, how He longs for us to be fully alert and engaged with the things that are on His heart at this present hour!

Prayer: *Lovely God, I receive Your exhortation to be watchful. I long to be with You wherever You are, investing my attention, time and energy into the things that grip Your heart. Open my eyes to see what You see, that I may be found in vigilant, watchful intercession, partnering with You as You move throughout the Earth.*

Day 6 – The Secret of Time

Psalm 119:32

I will run the course of Your commandments, for You shall enlarge my heart.

A friend recently told me, "The secret place has been the point of greatest frustration and attack in my personal walk." I know he's not alone. Since the secret place holds the keys to authentic overcoming in the Kingdom of God, the enemy will cause his strongest assaults to bear upon this single point of a Christian's life.

The full potential of the secret place with God requires one great overarching element: *time.* Lots of it. The more exclusive time you devote to Him, the more meaningful the relationship becomes.

There is a threshold to cross in terms of uncovering the full joy of the secret place. Until you find the threshold, you will find that you're consistently pushing yourself to get into the secret place, as though it's a burden instead of a joy. But once you cross the threshold, the secret place becomes a place of delight that you will gladly prioritize over the other competing demands. How do we cross that threshold? Give much time to the secret place. I never consider time invested in the secret place to be wasteful. Every hour invested is a filling up of the vial, and when it is full, the Lord will take us through the threshold into another dimension of delight and intimacy. But we'll never get there without investing *time.*

Satan wants you to believe that God is ticked at you because you haven't been meeting your daily quota of time with Him. He militates against the truth of God's Word, which states that our acceptance with God has to do with nothing but faith in Jesus Christ. God is very unimpressed with your performance, but He is deeply impressed with Christ's performance. When you put childlike faith in Christ, Christ's performance record is credited to you and the Father's heart is unlocked to you. When you believe on His beloved Son, the Father's heart explodes in affirmation, acceptance and delight—totally independent of your diligence or lack thereof.

As your heavenly Father and greatest fan, God is constantly coaxing you forward to the heights of spiritual victory. When you neglect the secret place, He's not disappointed *in* you, He's disappointed *for* you. He sees the spiritual riches available to you, and His heart breaks when He watches you getting by-passed. He wants you to share in Heaven's best, and He looks with wistful longing when you short-change yourself spiritually. Instead of feeling guilty, we should feel *ripped off*, then let lovesickness arise in our heart and exert whatever measure of spiritual violence is necessary to get our priorities back in line. The point is to carve out entire chunks of time that we can devote to long and loving meditation on the beauty and splendor of Christ Jesus our Lord.

Prayer: *Oh Lord, I love You so much; I am grieved at the way I've allowed the cares of this life to crowd You out. This has to stop, things have got to change. I miss drinking deeply of the Spirit's fountain. I miss being washed and cleansed and renewed in Your presence. I miss getting fed by the illumination of Your Word. I miss taking the time to calm my hectic heart and hear Your precious voice. I can't live without You! I've got to have more time with You! You are my very life and breath. Oh, I love You, Lord!*

Day 7 – The Secret of Journaling

Mark 4:24-25

Then [Jesus] said to them, "Take heed what you hear. With the same measure you use, it will be measured to you; and to you who hear, more will be given. For whoever has, to him more will be given; but whoever does not have, even what he has will be taken away from him."

I am fiercely committed to maintaining a spiritual journal, and it's for one all-encompassing reason: those who retain what God gives them will be given more (Mark 4:25). When I speak of a journal, I'm not talking about a personal diary. No, I'm referring to something far more consequential, deliberate and significant. It is the place where I chronicle the spiritual truths that are quickened to my spirit while I'm in the secret place.

I don't trust my brain. My memory is like a sieve. If I don't write it down, there's a 99% chance that I'll forget it. So when God reveals something valuable to me from His word, I don't trust myself to remember it. I write it down. He was kind enough to enlighten me with His truth, and now I must be a careful steward of that entrustment by retaining it, meditating upon it, and considering how that truth must impact how I live.

I keep a journal for one simple reason: I am desperate for more and because I am aware of my accountability before God. "For everyone to whom much is given, from him much will be required; and to whom much has been committed, of him they will ask more (Luke 12:48)." Look again at Mark 4:24-25. If we embrace God's Word to our hearts with great zeal, endeavoring to be a hearer *and* a doer of the Word, then He will measure out to us further insight with the same degree of diligence. But, as the passage also warns, if we are negligent with the insights God gives us, He will remove from our lives even that which we thought we had. I am personally convinced that I cannot hold on to what God gives me apart from writing it down. Journaling, then, is a vital element in being faithful before God.

I have made the vow of the psalmist my personal ambition: "I will not forget your word (Psalm 119:16)." When He feeds me with insight from His Word, I use every thinkable measure to retain that truth in my heart and soul incorporating it into the very fabric of my Christian experience and conduct. Here's my secret: I write it down and then review it every now and then.

Spiritual abundance is not a guarantee to all Believers; it is assured only to those who are faithful with what they receive (Luke 12:48; Matthew 13:12). So an abundant life in Christ is not passively received, it is aggressively taken.

Prayer: My God and my all! I am desperate for more! Continue to reveal Yourself to me so I can fall more in love with You. Let Your truth change who I am and how I live. May I be found as a good steward, faithful with all You have given me.

Day 8 – The Secret of Meditating

Joshua 1:8

This Book of the Law shall not depart from your mouth, but you shall meditate on it day and night, that you may observe to do according to all that is written in it. For then you will make your way prosperous, and then you will have good success.

What does it mean to meditate on God's Word? It means to slow way down the reading pace, and to contemplate every word and phrase, looking for deeper and fuller meanings. It's through meditation that we unlock the hidden riches of God's Word.

God's Word is like a mountain range with vast pockets of jewels and veins of gold. The secret place is our time to dig. We uncover various layers of rich understanding as we go deeper and deeper, pondering each word, and turning the phrases over and over in our mind. I always assume that every verse has more significance to it than I have yet discovered. Meditation is the art of digging out the most that we can from each and every word, diligently searching for fresh insights.

There is so much more depth to Scripture than what readily meets the eye at the first reading. Without His help we will never unlock the riches of His magnificent Word. Some truths will never be found until you take the time to sit and stare at the text, carefully considering its contents and implications. The one who meditates on God's Word will slowly transform the inner well from which his soul draws.

Jesus said, "A good man out of the good treasure of his heart brings forth good; and an evil man out of the evil treasure of his heart brings forth evil. For out of the abundance of the heart his mouth speaks (Luke 6:45)."

Once you become alive to the delight of meditating on God's Word, you'll become addicted. The secret place will become your favorite place, even moreso in some regards than the congregation of saints, because it's the place where Jesus feeds you personally. In church, you receive insights that have been processed first through another human channel. The sweetest morsels, however, are those which Jesus Christ gives directly to your own heart. When the Holy Spirit custom-fits the Word to your life circumstances, the sustaining power of His personalized word has the ability to carry you through great tribulations. This is the true fountain of life!

Prayer: *Father, I humbly admit my lack of understanding concerning Scripture. But I know that it is the wellspring of life, the source of wisdom and integrity, and a springboard that leads to encounters with You. I long to know You in a more profound way through Your Word, and I know You long to reveal Yourself to me. Drive me to the place of meditation by the hunger You incite in me. Make being with You in the secret place and gazing upon You in the Word to become my all-time favorite occupation in life. Kindle the fire of hunger in me. Draw me to Yourself, gracious Father!*

Day 9 – The Secret of Praying the Scriptures

Hebrews 4:12

For the word of God is living and powerful, and sharper than any two-edged sword, piercing even to the division of soul and spirit, and of joints and marrow, thoughts and intent of the heart.

The Bible is one massive Prayer Book. Virtually every page contains prayer prompts. As you take time to soak in His Word, not only is your meditation sweet, but you find yourself spontaneously expressing your heart back to God in response to the text.

Praying God's Word is powerful for several reasons:

- God's Word itself "is living and powerful (Hebrews 4:12)."
- When the language of our prayers is shaped by Scripture, we gain the confidence in knowing that we are praying according to will of God.
- As we pray God's Word back to Him, the language of His Word becomes the working language of our daily dialogue with him.
- We are equipped to pray according to the will of God in ways we would not have considered on our own.
- Praying the Scriptures adds a dimension of creativity and surprise to our prayer life, which in turn makes prayer much more fascinating and enjoyable.

As you pray the Scriptures, don't be afraid of repetition. The repetition of meaningful words and phrases works powerfully to lodge them in your spirit, and causes truth to have its full impact on your heart and mind. We want God's

Word to enter our hearts, grab our attention with its impact, enlarge and expand our hearts with passionate longing, become part of the fabric of our speech and actions, and bear fruit unto eternal life.

What a mighty gift God has given in His Word. He has given us a way to bypass the self-centered, human-based, pity-filled praying toward which our souls naturally gravitate. We can step into His mind, His thoughts, His expressions, His priorities, and pray according to His will from His Word in the power of the Holy Spirit. Awesome!

Prayer: *Wonderful God, Your Word is the light of my life. It exposes me unlike any other book in existence. You ordained every word so that it would guide me. Teach me to value Your Word over even my spiritual thinking. Reveal to me the wisdom of praying Your Word! Teach me to pray!*

Day 10 – The Secret of Boredom

Romans 8:26

Likewise the Spirit also helps in our weaknesses. For we do not know what we should pray for as we ought, but the Spirit Himself makes intercession for us with groaning which cannot be uttered.

Ever get bored while praying? If we're to be truthful, every one of us has been bored in the secret place. Even the twelve "apostles of the Lamb" fell asleep in the place of prayer (Matthew 26:40-45)! *Everybody gets bored in their personal prayer life and Bible reading.* There are some days when I seem to have an especially good connection with God. On those days, I often think, "Why isn't it like this all the time?" But in reality, there are a lot of deadpan days mixed in with the great ones. And I'm not alone. When I talk to others, I realize this is the common experience of weak human beings who, in their brokenness and frailty, are continually falling short of the kind of connection with God for which their heart yearns. "The spirit indeed is willing, but the flesh is weak (Jesus spoke those words directly related to prayer in Matthew 26:41)."

So what should we do when we're bored? Do it anyway. Persevere. Do the time. Grind it out. Allow nothing to dissuade or detour you, boredom included. Sometime along the way, we need to make a determined life decision: "By God's grace, I am devoting myself to the secret place, regardless of feelings or circumstances." And Christ will strengthen you in response to your sincere cries of, "Help!" When we are feeling especially weak, that's the time to reach out to Him for the abundance of His grace.

I am writing this chapter primarily to defuse the enemy's scheme to burden you with guilt and shame in regards to your secret life with God. He tries to tell you that you're a failure or a hypocrite when, in reality, you're walking the same pilgrimage that the greatest saints of history have traversed before you. To put it bluntly, sometimes prayer is boring and Bible reading is like eating sawdust. But here's the good part: *one day of exhilaration in the Holy Spirit is worth a thousand days of struggle!* Once God touches you with His Spirit and energizes you with His Word, you're hopelessly hooked. You don't care how long this desert might last; you're going to keep walking because you know that on the other side is an oasis of heavenly delights.

Now here's even better news: *as you persevere in the secret place, the very nature of your relationship with the Lord begins to change—and the bad days get fewer and further in between!* There's a threshold to cross in which, once you cross it, the thrill of the secret place grabs your spirit and you gain unparalleled momentum in connecting with God. The point is, if you stay with it, eventually the breakthrough will come. There may be boring hours in between, but don't quit. The greatest things in life—those things that carry eternal value—always come at the steepest price. And boredom is such a small price to pay for having the chance to gaze upon the most lovely Being in existence.

Prayer: *My loving God, I can't help but be honest with You... sometimes I deal with feelings of guilt and shame because I am bored or weary in my devotional time with You. Oh, how my soul longs for You in that dry and weary land where there is no spiritual water! Respond to my cry for help. Holy Spirit I need You! Lord, let me feel the warmth of Your nearness once again. Touch my cold, bored heart with the fire of Your love. Take me beyond the threshold into profound intimacy with You! By Your grace, I will persevere!*

Day 11 – The Secret of Feeling Attractive to God

Song of Solomon 4:7, 9

All beautiful you are, my darling; there is no flaw in you...
You have stolen my heart, my sister, my bride; you have
stolen my heart with one glance of your eyes.

When you come before God, how do you think He sees you? Your answer to that question is vitally important to the success of your secret life with God.

Nothing is deadlier to the secret place than a false idea of how God views you; and nothing is more powerfully energizing than when your mind is renewed in the Word of God and you come to understand how He sees you. The Accuser wants you to see a Father who is harsh, demanding, never satisfied with your performance, mostly disappointed with you, and frustrated with the slow rate of your spiritual growth. This false idea of how God views you will drive your emotional response to Him. You will be wearied with trying to please Him and your spirit will not soar in the liberty of loving adoration that He has designed for you. *But when you gain ownership of the fact that God is smiling on you, that He is desiring your company and that He longs to be intimate with you, then the truth of that reality starts to touch your emotional chemistry and you actually begin to feel attractive to God!*

It all starts with understanding how God feels about the cross of Christ. Revelation 5:6 describes Jesus as a Lamb standing before the eternal throne "as though [He] had been slain." In other words, the death of Christ is as fresh to God's mind as the day it happened. Time will never erase from before God's eyes the immediacy and the horror of Calvary, and the powerful atoning work of the blood of Christ. God is eternally and infinitely passionate about His

Son's cross! Those who place their faith in Christ's great sacrifice of love unlock the infinite passion and delight of an exuberant God who yearns to be joined to your heart in eternal affection. He doesn't enjoy you any less because you struggle. He knows your weaknesses, He sees your failures, but yet He enjoys you even when you fall! He loves it when you pick yourself up and keep stepping forward again into His arms as His child. He enjoys us at every stage of the maturity process. You don't have to wonder if He wants you to come into the secret place. He has been waiting for you, and He'll continue to wait for as long as necessary—because His heart is wrapped up in your life.

This understanding has the power to change *everything* about how you relate to God. When you know you're attractive to God, you come into His presence with boldness—the way He wants you to—with a lifted face, with expectant eyes, with a delighted smile, with an eager voice, and with a burning heart. Psalm 45:11 tells how our beloved Lord feels when He looks at us: "So the King will greatly desire your beauty." This is how the King looks at His Bride who has left everything in order to be joined to her Husband. *You are stunningly beautiful to Jesus!* When He looks upon your beauty, He longs to have you and hold you forever and ever. When you come to the secret place, you are coming into the chamber of the King who finds you both beautiful and desirable. Not only do you long for His presence, He longs for yours!

Prayer: Oh Jesus, speak Your strong love to my weak heart! Let me know that Your affections are fastened upon me. Tell me once more that I am the passion of Your heart. I want to be joined to You in love! Let me feel Your delight and enjoyment of me, even in my weakness. Yes, I am darkened by sin, but I am lovely to You. I long to come into Your presence with the confidence that comes from feeling the affections of Your heart toward me. Tell me how beautiful I am to You, my wonderful Bridegroom!

Day 12 – The Secret of Enduring

Philippians 3:12, 14

Not that I have already attained, or am already perfected; but I press on, that I may lay hold of that for which Christ Jesus has also laid hold of me. I press toward the goal for the prize of the upward call of God in Christ Jesus.

As we poise ourselves for the full marathon of the Christian race, not only must we gather our daily manna, we must also grow in the Christlike quality of *endurance*. We all have desert seasons with God when everything in our spiritual life is dry, dusty and void of inspiration. More than just boredom or a bad day, I'm speaking of a significant amount of time—a season—in the wilderness. The only way through is to make a decision ahead of time that no matter how tough the slogging gets, you're never going to give up on your pursuit of God. You're going to abide in Christ no matter what. I'll let you in on a secret: this kind of tenacious commitment to endurance will open the path to the most meaningful dimensions of relationship with the Lord.

Seasons not only break the monotony of sameness, they are necessary to productivity. Nothing can live in non-stop sunshine; this only creates a desert. Night is as important as day; the sun must be followed by clouds and rain. It's easy to endure in good times. It's when the hard times hit that our faithful endurance is proven. We don't enjoy storms, but they are an essential part of a complete life, and the key to victory comes in finding how to weather the storms of life in such a way that they don't dislodge us from our secret life in God.

Hardship can be embraced with joy, in my opinion, only when we understand God's purpose in the pain. "My Brethren, count it all joy when you fall into various trials, *knowing* that the testing of your faith produces patience (James 1:2-3)." The only way to be joyful in trials is through *knowing*—knowing God's purpose in it. How do we learn God's purposes in our sufferings? The secret pursuit of God in His Word and an active encounter of His presence is what will reveal purpose to us. *The sanctuary of His embrace is where God reveals His purpose, which in turn empowers us to endure hardship with joy for we know He is working it all together for good* (Romans 8:28). One of the greatest challenges in the place of hardship is to suffer *with joy*. It's not possible in human strength! Which is why Paul prayed that they might be "strengthened with all might," for it takes the might of God to rejoice through long durations of painful hardship. Simply put, godly endurance is impossible apart from a well-nurtured secret life with God.

Don't ever give up! Instead, set your heart and energy into pursuing His purpose behind whatever season you find yourself in. The Lord will always give you the grace and strength to overcome in each season as He leads you through. Today may be the day when He rewards your devotion with an overwhelming revelation of the eternal glory of the Man Christ Jesus, our Lord! Through the might of God's Spirit, *any* hardship can be endured with joy for the extravagance of such a reward.

Prayer: *Patient and gracious Lord, I give my love to You here and now. I commit my energy to seek for Your joy and grace in the secret place amidst suffering and hardship. May I find the knowledge of God, the beauty of Your majesty and Your loving, wise purposes in this place of sacrifice and joy. Strengthen my heart with the hope of finding Your purposes.*

Day 13 – The Secret of Waiting

Psalm 27:14

Wait on the Lord; be of good courage, and He shall strengthen your heart; wait, I say, on the Lord.

The secret place is a time machine, transporting us from our time zone to His. Here we step into the eternal and begin to view all of life from the perspective of the Ageless One who is without beginning or ending of days. From this vantage point, waiting on God takes on an entirely different hue. The closer you get to God, the more you realize He's in no hurry. *There is no frenetic hurrying in Heaven, only calculated purpose.* Those who step into God's time zone will not allow urgent matters to press them into acting too quickly and getting ahead of God.

Someone once said, "We should seek His face and not His hand." I disagree. We seek His face *and* His hand. We seek the intimacy of His face, but we also seek the power of His hand. It's not either/or; it's both/and. We so long for the release of His power that we gaze with rapt attention upon Him until He moves on our behalf.

Waiting on God may be the most difficult of all the spiritual disciplines, and perhaps that's the reason so few truly practice it. Waiting on God is not watching television until God chooses to move; it is attentively gazing upon Him with undistracted focus until He has mercy on us. And until He does act, we just wait on Him and love Him. Just sitting in His presence and gazing... it can be agonizing to us who have become accustomed to being bombarded with data and stimuli. We lack the attention span to wait on God. But He knows that, so in His kindness He designs scenarios that will help us learn how to wait on Him. *Once we press through and cross the boredom threshold, our hearts open to the joys and adventures of waiting on God.*

To wait on God successfully, we must come to derive more fulfillment by being with Him than by working for Him. When being with Him fully satisfies us, we can wait for as long as necessary—just as long as He stays with us.

Prayer: *Awesome Father, I admit my anxiousness and unwillingness to wait upon You. But I know that everything You do is infused with divine purpose. I don't want to get ahead of You or Your timing in any area of my life. Take me beyond the threshold of being bored with waiting on You! I set aside the human weakness that finds it easier to work for You than to simply be with You. Satisfy the longings of my heart to be with You. Set me ablaze with Your fiery passion that I might wait upon You with holy zeal and fiery ecstasy.*

Day 14 – The Secret of Tears

Psalm 42:3

My tears have been my food day and night, while they continually say to me, "Where is your God?"

One of the greatest gifts you can bring to your King is the gift of absolute sincerity. I'm talking about a purity of heart that says, "Lord, I'm coming to You because You really are the center of my universe. You truly are all that I live for. My heart is totally and fully set upon You." Nothing surpasses the delight of being able to sing songs of total consecration with absolute abandon. Oh what delight when we can come boldly before His throne with a clean conscience! Even though we're not yet perfected and even though we struggle with weakness, our hearts reach for Him with impassioned desire.

I have personally found my awareness of His presence to be strongest when I have had great yearning of heart for Him. *When my soul longs for Him in sweet sincerity, even to tears, my awareness of His reciprocating affections is heightened.*

True love must function in total sincerity, void of duplicity or adulterous passions. This is why we must find those measures that evoke our sense of sweet sincerity before the Lord. Now, here's the beauty of it: *when love is without hypocrisy, the sweetness of this sincerity is often accompanied by tears.* David cried, "Do not be silent at my tears (Ps. 39:12)," as though his tears proved his sincerity.

There's something about tears that is pure and unfeigned. I suppose it's possible, in a technical sense, to fake tears (as actors learn to do), but let's be honest about it, nobody is about to fake tears while praying in their secret place; in that place, tears are either honest, or they're absent.

We cry because we desire or because we're in pain; so tears are the language of desire. We desire Him, even to tears. If we lack that desire, He will cultivate it within us by seemingly withdrawing from us in His mercy. *It's famine that makes us hungry; it's drought that makes us thirsty. Deprivation produces desire.* So do not despise the pain that gave you tears. Pour out your heart to him; God is a refuge for us! Those who "love much" still wash the Lord's feet with their tears (see Luke 7:36-48). Weeping and tears have always gained the Lord's attention. Not only does the Lord notice our tears, He actually bottles and stores them as an everlasting witness in His presence (Ps. 56:8).

There are two kinds of "sickness" in the Bible that produce tears. The first is heartsickness. When the hope of God's deliverance is deferred, the heart grows sick (Pr. 13:12), and a groan arises from the depths of your spirit that is expressed with tears. The other "sickness" that produces tears is seen in Song of Solomon 5:8, "...if you find my beloved, tell him I am lovesick!" Lovesickness is the consequence of our Lord's restrained self-revelation. When the heart is awakened to the beauty of the King and the eyes long to behold Him, but He reveals Himself in but a fraction of His fullness, the saint becomes sick with love. *Heartsickness is the product of unrequited power; lovesickness is the product of unrequited love.* David articulated both passions when, during his years of hiding in the wilderness, he cried, "So I have looked for You in the sanctuary, to see *Your power* and *Your glory* (Ps. 63:2)." *Heartsickness weeps, "Show me Your hand!" Lovesickness weeps, "Show me Your face!"* The inner chamber of prayer gains its impetus from the liquid power of tears.

The presence of tears is a profound statement to your departed Bridegroom. *Tears are liquid words.* Tears say more than words often can. Whereas words can sometimes contain pretense of plastic platitudes, tears come straight from the heart. Have you known tears? Then you are blessed. Do you struggle to find tears? Then ask for them. It's a request He will graciously fulfill.

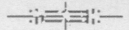

Prayer: *Holy Father, I love You—You know that I do. I am a child reaching to You for help and grace. In Your great mercy, do whatever it takes to compel me to greater depth in my relationship with You. My heart has not felt what You feel; I do not weep enough over my own sin with the same emotions that You have. Break the hardness of my heart and give me the sweet sincerity that I long for! Come, faithful and merciful God, with the power to deliver me, and show me Your love! Restrain Yourself from me so I will chase after You; reveal Yourself to me so I will chase after You! Make me heartsick and lovesick to the point that I refuse to go without you! I love You, my God!*

Day 15 – The Secret of Inviting His Gaze

Psalm 11:4, 5, 7

The Lord is in His holy temple, the Lord's throne is in Heaven; His eyes behold, His eyelids test the sons of men. The Lord tests the righteous, but the wicked and the one who loves violence His soul hates... For the Lord is righteous, He loves righteousness; His countenance beholds the upright.

We can do nothing to avoid His gaze; however, it is possible to invite Him to an even greater attentiveness of our lives. Why would we want to do such a thing? Simply because His gaze is reflective of His favor. He looks with favor upon the upright.

The Lord has said to us, "But on this one will I look: on him who is poor and of contrite spirit, and who trembles at My word (Isaiah 66:2)." When I read those words my heart moves within me, "That's me Lord, I'm poor and contrite, and I tremble at Your word. Oh, that You would look upon me in this way!"

God is on a holy search. "For the eyes of the Lord run to and fro throughout the whole Earth, to show Himself strong on behalf of those whose heart is loyal to Him (2 Corinthians 16:9)." God is looking for the hungry and loyal heart, and when He finds it, His eyes cease their searching, and they bare down with great fascination and excitement upon the one who loves Him so devoutly. Those who come under such intense scrutiny gain great favor from the Lord. He releases abundant portions of mercy, faith, grace, compassion, revelation, wisdom, might and deliverance to those whose heart is loyal to Him. *Wise Believers—those who have come to value the true treasures of the Kingdom—will pant for this kind of attention.*

Here's the tricky part: with His favor comes His fire. When He looks upon you for good, it is with eyes ablaze. His fiery eyes can't but test you. God's fire is heartwarming and impassioning, but it's also calculatedly volatile and dangerously consuming. When God's fire explodes in your life, you can rest assured He is beholding you very closely. He is testing your every response to see if your heart will remain loyal to Him through the scrutiny. If you persevere, He designs to show Himself strong on your behalf (2 Chronicles 16:9). I have had such sweet meditation in considering the intense concentration of God's attention upon our lives. He is more focused on me, even though I am one among billions, than I could ever be capable of reciprocating. When my mind wanders from a conscious focus upon the Lord, and I am distracted by the affairs of everyday life, upon returning to Christ in my thoughts comes this awesome realization: He was there all along, waiting for my thoughts to return to Him! He never disconnected or got distracted away from me, not even for a split-second.

There is a place of rich affection where, in the quiet of our secret garden, we invoke the gaze of our Beloved. A resolute heart gains the Lord's extravagant response, "You have ravished My heart, My sister, My spouse; you have ravished My heart with one look of your eyes (Song of Solomon 4:9)." Eyes locked, hearts burning... this is the secret place.

Prayer: Jesus, look upon me with Your great favor and be merciful to me! Fix Your loving gaze upon my life. Search me and test me. I invite the wisdom of Your testing to have its way in my life and to run its complete course. Leave no part of my heart untouched by Your fiery gaze. Show Yourself strong on my behalf as my heart grows in faithfulness to You. Before You, I am poor and contrite of spirit, trembling merely at Your word. Set Your gaze upon me, my dear Lord!

Day 16 – The Secret of the Cross

Psalm 91:1

He who dwells in the secret place of the Most High shall abide under the shadow of the Almighty.

We must return to the cross intentionally and continually. You cannot draw closer to the shadow of God Almighty than when you are hugging the cross. *The cross's shadow is the saint's home.* It is the safest place on Earth. It is the place where the most violent winds will whip across your soul, but also where you will enjoy the greatest immunity from Satan's devices. By embracing the cross, you are dying to every mechanism in your soul that Satan could use against you. There is no strategy against crucified saints because they do not love their lives even unto death.

We know that we are crucified with Christ (Galatians 2:20), but "self" has an uncanny way of crawling off the cross and asserting itself. The crucifixion of the self-life is not an achievement, but a process. As Gethsemane's garden of prayer prepared Jesus to embrace His cross, the secret place is where we reiterate our *yes* to the Father to suffer according to His will. Permit me to explain what I mean here when I say "suffering." In our daily pilgrimage to the secret place, we wrap ourselves around His rugged tree, gaze upon His wounds, and once again die to ourselves. We allow the suffering of the flesh to cleanse us from sin (Colossians 1:24).

Many people see the cross as the place of pain and restriction, and that is true. But it is so much more! The cross is the place of absolute love. The cross is the Father saying to the world, "This is how much I love you!" The cross is the Son saying to the Father, "This is how much I love You!" And the cross is the Bride saying to her Bridegroom, "This is how much I love You!" The cross is consummate passion poured forth. When Christ calls us to share His cross, He invites us to the highest intimacy.

As you hang with Him here, even though your vision is clouded and you cannot see His face, if you listen, you will hear His voice. With passionate, determined, hope-filled words He will guide you through this dark night of your soul. Jesus gently coaches you to abandon yourself completely to the hands of your beloved Father. *As you lay down your life, He takes the profound death that has worked itself in you and transforms it into resurrection life. You are joined to Christ in His death, in His burial and in His resurrection!* Unparalleled affection is reserved for those who share this cross with their Beloved. This *is* the secret place. Here exchanged are the fathomless passions of the Eternal God with His select partner. Nothing can separate these two— neither death nor life, nor height nor depth. They do it all together. Their hearts are forever entwined in the passion story of the universe. This is extravagant love—no length spared, no part withheld—for the cross empowers total abandonment. Every *yes* of this secret place fuels renewed exchange of exclusive devotion. Anything for love!

Come aside to the desolate hill of crucifixion. Say yes once more. Join your suffering Savior. Drink of His cup—all of it. And discover the secret of everlasting love in the shadow of the Almighty.

***

Prayer: Jesus, I have been too far from the shadow of Your cross! I long for a greater revelation of You... to know Your power and Your servanthood, Your love and Your justice. Open this doorway of understanding to me—this extravagant love, this exclusive devotion, this place of significance that the cross holds in Your heart. Show me how to abandon myself completely to the faithful hands of my Father as You did. Open my ears to what You are saying through the cross and show me how to join You in it. I will draw near and join myself to You alone!

Day 17 – The Secret of Rest

Mark 6:31

He said to them, "Come aside by yourselves to a deserted place and rest a while."

The journey gets long for all of us. Every one of us, without exception, needs to find that place of coming aside to be refreshed in the place of rest.

Jesus said that He came to give us rest (Matthew 11:28), and yet we Christians are some of the most worn-out people on the planet. There is a rest that remains for God's people, but it's very possible to miss it. God's rest is available but not guaranteed. There's something we must do to enter this rest (Hebrews 4:11).

Those who neglect the secret place always seem to struggle with stress and demands. Their lives tend toward a constant flurry of incessant activity. Jesus designed that there be a portion of our day when we just STOP; *stop the frenetic pace, get off the merry-go-round, and calm our hearts in the love of God.*

God's rest is uncovered through a diligent pursuit of the secret place. The rest of God can be found only in ceasing from all our own works and learning to just "be" in the presence of the Lord (Hebrews 4:10). Here is our source of rejuvenation, revitalization, invigoration and renewal.

What could be more energizing in the course of a busy day than to stop and gaze upon the glory of His enthroned majesty?

Instead of tiring from your service to God, you can actually be energized and made alive by it. But it is only in understanding that spending time in His presence does not diminish our productivity in life, but rather becomes the wellspring from which flows Spirit-empowered effectiveness and fruitfulness. It is the only abode of true rest.

⁓ :¦⸗¦: ⁓

Prayer: *Jesus, You are the Prince of Peace. I ask that You continue to cause the hunger in me to grow even more; strengthen the desire in my heart to come aside with You, surrendering the burdens and stresses of my daily life. I know it takes the drawing work of Your Spirit to fall deeper in love with You, so I ask You to draw me to Yourself. I invite You to reach into the depths of my heart and cause me to long for You just as You long for me. Take me away with You, my beloved God! Cause me to find my greatest rest in Your overwhelming love.*

Day 18 – The Secret of The Refuge

Psalm 27:5

For in the time of trouble He shall hide me in His pavilion; in the secret place of His tabernacle He shall hide me; He shall set me high upon a rock.

Storms will unavoidably assault us on this earthly plane, but there *is* a place to hide, where God hides His beloved ones—in the sanctuary of His presence. The Refuge (I'm referring to the secret place, of course) is an asylum for the war-weary soldier, a place of immunity from the poachings of the enemy.

In Psalm 63:1, David wrote, "So I have looked for You in the *sanctuary*, to see Your power and Your glory." But when he wrote that psalm, he was isolated, a political fugitive, hiding in the wilderness, and being hunted by King Saul—David was nowhere near a sanctuary. I believe he was referring to his secret life with God. Even though he couldn't worship before the ark, he discovered the secret place to be a shelter from the swirl of emotions and troubles that constantly bombarded his soul. Here he could vent his anxious thoughts; here he could be renewed in God's love as he gazed on His beauty; here he could be quieted by the assurances of his heavenly Father's protection; here he was healed from the wounds of man's rejection; here he regained strength for the journey; here he was safe.

Yet, *while the secret place is a place of immunity, it is also one of Satan's favorite places to attack the devout.* When we retreat to the secret place, the storm doesn't mysteriously dissipate. For example, Daniel's detractors attacked him on the grounds of his prayer life. Judas chose to betray Jesus at Jesus' place of prayer. The assurance to the Believer, however, is that when you are attacked in the place of prayer, the Father is exercising sovereign jurisdiction over the entire affair. *Nothing can happen to you in the secret place that He doesn't specifically allow for His higher purposes.* You are totally immune to anything outside His will.

The closer we draw to the Lord in intimacy, the more real the warfare will be that we encounter. As the attacks increase, our cry only intensifies, "Hide me!" While the body and soul may be afflicted with increasing harassment and abuse, the spirit is finding a place of greater protection, rest and intimacy under the shadow of the Almighty (see 2 Corinthians 4:8-11). The Spirit thus draws us into a place of greater spiritual peace and comfort which only inflames the soul with a greater passion for Jesus—which in turn only feeds the ire of our tormentors. But waiting on God until the deliverance comes can be agonizing at times (the fact that God delivers us from those things does not negate the reality of the pain we experience when we are initially caught in their grip).

Though we may suffer, there is deliverance—and that deliverance is found in the secret place, the place of refuge. May you have the grace to make the decision now: lose your life and pursue the secret place of the Most High. It is where we sustain the greatest assaults, but there's no safer place in the universe to be.

Prayer: *Thank You, Lord, for the gift of the secret place! You are my deliverer, my strength, the one who loves to show Himself strong for me! Give me the grace to make You my Refuge daily. Through pain or victory, intimacy or warfare, may I seek to encounter You above all else. I love You, my Lord!*

Day 19 – The Secret of Beholding Jesus

Luke 24:32

Did not our hearts burn within us while He talked with us on the road, and while He opened the Scriptures to us?

Some readers come to the Bible to gain insight or to learn truths and principles. However, coming to the Bible with only your mind can leave your heart untouched. There is so much more to gain from Scripture than just truth about God. You can gain God Himself! The true riches are found in beholding and knowing the Lord Jesus Christ; the true riches are "bought" at the price of spending time at the feet of Jesus and hearing His word during an encounter with Him. And that's where the secret place comes in! It's here—with the Word open before us, with hearts tenderized by the Spirit, and with a spiritual appetite that pants for the food of Heaven—that we peer into the beauties of holiness in order to see Him more clearly and know His ways.

The Pharisees made a deadly error in how they approached the Scriptures. They dissected Scripture cognitively, but they didn't seek the heart behind the truths revealed, and thus they came to know the Book, but not the Author. This is what Jesus meant when He said to them, "You *search the Scriptures*, for in them you think you have eternal life; and these are they which testify of Me. *But you are not willing to come to Me* that you may have life (John 5:39-40, emphasis added)." People of understanding will seek to *encounter God* rather than just read about Him.

The Scriptures have always been intended to direct our hearts to a Person. The entire purpose of the Old Testament was to enflame the hearts of God's people for the beauty of His face. They got hung up, however, on dogma and creed and missed the living relationship that God longed to have with them. *Jesus' numerous rebukes to the Pharisees raise a frightening possibility; we can read the Bible avidly and never get to know the Lord.* It's the opening of the Scriptures concerning Christ to the thirsty soul, through the power of the Holy Spirit, that creates the burning heart. This is the great pursuit of the secret place!

My experience has been that I don't get to know Jesus better in prayer. Prayer is where I express my love according to how I have *already* come to know Him. Prayer is love exchanged. *But if I am to come to know Him better, I must approach His Word and behold Him there. To know more of Christ requires revelation, and revelation usually requires meditation in the Word.*

I've discovered that I am naturally attracted to that which is different from me (as the saying goes, opposites attract.) Jesus is stunning in His singular beauty and matchless majesty. And, oh, what a privilege I have—to come to the secret place and gaze upon Him in the Scriptures, forever fascinated with the adventure of growing in the knowledge of Him who loved me and fought for my love unto death!

Prayer: My Altogether Lovely God, I long to behold You! Give me the glorious privilege of ever gazing upon Your beauty. This is how I want to live my life: no matter where I go or what I do, let my face be fastened upon the throne to behold Your radiance, my beloved Lord. Manifest Yourself to me! This unfulfilled desire causes me to be lovesick—and may I never recover from this holy dissatisfaction! Cause my heart to burn by allowing me to gaze upon You!

Day 20 – The Secret of Standing

Deuteronomy 10:8

At that time the Lord separated the tribe of Levi to bear the Ark of the Covenant of the Lord, to stand before the Lord, to minister to Him and to bless in His name, to this day.

When you retreat to the secret place, you are standing in the Spirit together with all the saints on the sea of glass and gazing upon the One who is seated on the throne (Revelation 15:2). Even though your eyes are veiled so you can't see Him with the natural eye, you are still standing directly before the throne! The highest privilege of all creation is to stand before the living fire of God's presence and burn with holy affections for your Father and King. In the secret place we simply stand; no great agenda, no mighty ambitions, no rush to move on to the next "big thing." We just stand before Him and love Him. Standing here is your eternal destiny, and you can taste a bit of Heaven on Earth by shutting your door and standing before your God in the beauty of holiness.

Accept this... no, more than just acceptance, *embrace this marvelous secret*: there are seasons when God calls us to simply stand; and it is wise. We might prefer the adrenaline rush or notoriety of chasing down a great cause, but sometimes God calls us to stop all activity and just stand. Sometimes He gives us no choice. Occasionally, circumstances will constrain us beyond our ability to steer a different course, and we become prisoners to the chains that bind us to God's will. Incapable of extricating ourselves and moving on to the next thing, all we can do is stand and burn in holy love for our King.

I've discovered that sometimes God is divinely, purposefully wasteful; and it is wise. The Scripture shows us that God has mighty angels who stand in His presence, in some cases for hundreds of years, and wait for His bidding. With all their strength and might, God just has them standing around the throne waiting on Him! If it were a matter of strength, God has all the strength in Heaven He needs! And, then the Holy Spirit whispered to me, "I don't need your strength." It wasn't the strength of the eternal Son that bought our redemption; it was the fact that He was crucified in weakness, bringing us salvation. God doesn't need our strength, He needs our availability. He's just looking for us to stand in His presence, gaze upon Him, and fulfill His words when He speaks; *this is wisdom.* Are you between assignments? Then just stand before Him, enjoy Him and let Him enjoy you.

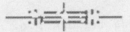

Prayer: *God of Wisdom, I come humbly before You to repent. It is so easy for me to get swept up into doing things for You, rather than allowing You to sweep me away in love. My heart is so bent towards getting praise from people that I sometimes neglect the privilege of simply standing before You and giving You my love. Please forgive me and grant me the wisdom enough to seek You first above all things. If I do nothing else for You, I will stand in Your presence to minister to You. Make my heart a holy flame of love that burns only for You. Give me passion first and then zeal, my wonderful God.*

Day 21 – The Secret of Just Loving Him

Song of Songs 3:4

...I found the one I love. I held Him and would not let Him go...

From the devotional yesterday, you may be wondering, "What is the point of *just standing?*" This is the answer to that question and possibly the entire summation of the secret place: it is *to encounter in love.* I cannot emphasize this enough. So please read the previous sentence again and again and again, until it sinks in.

God gave His only begotten Son, and Jesus died an excruciating death all for love. The central reason for this whole thing between God and man is love! *Jesus died for one all-encompassing reason, that He might manifest the graciousness of His glorious love to us, and reap the extravagant affections of a lovesick Bride in return.* He did it all for love!

Love is the primary staple of the secret place. So you'll often find yourself spending most of your quiet time in the simple exchange of affection. You'll find a thousand and more ways to say, "I love you," and He'll amaze you with the creativity and energy with which He'll reciprocate His passions for you.

Start your day with just loving Him; *encounter Him in love.* Your requests can wait; your Bible studying can wait; your intercession can wait. Before anything else, give your love to your Lord. Let Him know that love is the great motivator of your heart. "I'm here, Father, because I love You. You are the center of my universe! I hallow and reverence Your name. I enjoy being with You."

The Lord has put His requirements within easy reach of every one of us, regardless of social class, age, personality, giftings, etc. All He asks is that you *encounter Him in love*. Love is the great equalizer in the Kingdom, putting us all on the same playing field. No one has an advantage over another in giving and receiving love. The secret place is where we seek to become a better lover of God. We practice the language of love; we search for ways to give even more of our hearts to Him in love. This has nothing to do with your personality. Just come and love Him. He's looking for heartfelt sincerity, for visceral passion, for authentic relationship—*for an encounter of love.*

Love is the most powerful force in the universe. *When you simply release your love to the Lord, you are stepping into the dimension where God works on behalf of His beloved ones.* There is no greater spiritual warfare, no better intercession, and no winning battle that could possibly compare. Just love Him and you'll unlock "the reckless, raging fury that they call the love of God (song lyrics by Rich Mullins)," He will fight your battles, and you'll be lifted into new dimensions of blessed communion with Your Lover and Friend. When you encounter Jesus in love, you will not be denied or let down!

Prayer: Jesus, my Lover, come to me and bring Your great love! Touch my heart once again. I long for a real encounter with You, not just a time of study. I know I have not sought You to the extent that I would like to think I have, but I ask You to touch my weak heart and strengthen me to pursue You. I love You, God—You know I do—strengthen me with Your love! Touch my heart with Your great passion and I will be energized to run after You. Draw me into the hidden places of desire that are in Your heart. I long to be swept away by You!

Day 22 – The Secret of Bodily Light

Luke 11:33-36

No one, when he has lit a lamp, puts it in a secret place or under a basket, but on a lampstand, that those who come in may see the light. The lamp of the body is the eye. Therefore, when your eye is good, your whole body is also is full of light. But when your eye is bad, your whole body also is full of darkness. Therefore take heed that the light which is in you is not darkness. If then your whole body is full of light, having no part dark, the whole body will be full of light, as when the bright shining lamp gives you light.

We know that Jesus came to give us light in our spirit, soul and understanding. Please consider with me, though, the truth that He also came to give us light in our body.

It's fascinating that Jesus spoke of our bodies as though they can be filled with either light or darkness. The implications of this truth are vitally important to our victory and joy in Christ, and intensely relevant to our secret place.

There is a place in God where our bodies are full of light, where all darkness has been eradicated from our bodies. This is a place of incredible freedom from temptation because temptation often finds its power in the fact that it is able to appeal to darkness within us. *When the body is full of light, bodily sins lose their power over us, and we walk in a fantastic dimension of victory.* When I speak of bodily sins I am referring to sins that we commit with our bodies, such as drunkenness, gluttony, fornication, masturbation, viewing pornography, illegal drug use, murder, gossip, stealing, lying, slander, coarse language, and many, many other things.

If we come to the secret place with a clear and healthy eye, the light of God's Word will penetrate every facet of our lives, our bodies included, and we will become filled with light in every part of our being. A good eye brings light into the body; a bad eye will keep light out. The whole thing has to do with the eyes. It is vitally important what we look at! If we peer into the God's Word, we will be filled with illumination and clarity; if we look at things that defile, we not only fill our minds with garbage, but we also allow darkness to get established in portions of our body.

When our eye is bad, we can come to God's Word and still not see anything. Then how do we get a good eye? As we apply ourselves to God's Word in a disciplined, focused way, our eye will slowly begin to heal and clear up, and will begin to let the light of Christ into our bodies (Psalm 19:8).

But victory over sin is not the greatest reward of a body filled with light. Of far greater significance is the intimacy we find with Christ. When our body is filled with light, our body has come into full alignment with God's Kingdom and purposes (1 Corinthians 6:13-20). There is nothing within our bodies that is resisting His will.

Have you ever wondered why it takes so long to engage your heart with God and get to a place where you feel spiritually ready to commune with God? We all deal with feelings of shame, guilt or unworthiness. But maybe a starting place to overcome these areas is with the eyes. Child of God, what are you looking at? The answer to that question may be a large piece of the breakthrough you so earnestly desire. When we are in the daily grind and allowing all manner of darkness into our eyes, it just makes sense that we would experience difficulty with entering into God's presence quickly. But when you come to worship the Lord with a body full of light, you don't need a "warm up" period before you finally engage with God; you are ready at a moment's notice to soar in the spirit with your Beloved.

When your body is filled with light, you will know greater victory over bodily sins, you will touch deeper dimensions of intimacy with Jesus, and you will be granted a place of greater influence in the Body of Christ. Guard your eyes, dearly beloved! Give your eyes to reading His Word and beholding His face. Then, when you are tempted, your body will not be fighting against your spirit. Your body will be in alignment with the light, and the tentacles of lust and greed and anger will not be able to wrap around and enslave you. Put a guard on your eyes, reserving them to behold the glory of God and look into His wonderful Word. Then your entire being will radiate the light and glory of God.

Prayer: *Lovely Lord, You are the light of all the world, including my life. I honor You as my Creator and my King, and I love You as my Friend and Bridegroom! Wicked darkness surrounds me on every side—it even invades the deep places of my heart when I lose sight of You. How I wish that would never happen! You know how weak I am and where I need strength. Holy Spirit, search me and expose my darkness. Let Your light and Your truth guide me. Grip me with how jealous You are about how I spend my time and where I set my gaze. Fill me with light so that I may delight Your heart. Faithful One, draw me to Yourself.*

Day 23 – The Secret of Being Known

1 Corinthians 8:3

But if anyone loves God, this one is known by Him.

Someone once asked, "Do you know God?" But there's a question that is far more important: does God know you? The issue on the great Day of Judgment will not be whether you know God but whether God knows you.

Many will claim to know God in the Day of Judgment. They will say to Him, "Lord, Lord, I know you! I have prophesied in Your name, cast out demons in Your name and done many wonders in Your name. I ate and drank in Your presence, and taught about You in our streets. I swear I *do* know You!"

But to some of them He will reply, "I don't know you and I don't know where you're from. In fact, I *never* knew you. Depart from Me, you who practice lawlessness (See Matthew 7:21-23 and Luke 13:25-27)!" How horrifying to *think* you know God, only to discover that He doesn't know you! The issues at risk here are of eternal consequence. There can be no question that is more fundamentally important than this: what must I do to be known by God?

The answer has everything to do with my secret life with God. *He wants me to enter the secret place, sit before Him, remove every façade and mask of pretense, and reveal to Him the innermost places of my heart.* He wants me to unveil my face before Him (2 Corinthians 3:18) and let Him see the real me. He wants me to love Him without holding back any part of my being. He wants a relationship with me that is based on total transparency and honesty. I am changing more and more into the image of Christ, but during the process I allow Him to see the naked truth of my brokenness and carnality.

God does know everything about us already, but just because He sees certain dark rooms in our hearts doesn't mean we've invited His light into those dark rooms. The human tendency is to hide and cover up. If we try to hide our true condition from Him, not only do we deceive ourselves, but we also hold ourselves back from being known by Him. *When He says He knows us, He means that we have invited Him into every part of our thoughts, motives, desires and actions.* And when we invite Him in, He releases His grace to empower us to overcome sinful patterns that had previously seemed unconquerable. As a negative example, Judas Iscariot illustrates the terrifying truth that it's possible to spend lots of time in the presence of Jesus and still not invite Him into the secrets of your heart.

Jesus can handle the confessions of our actual struggles; what He can't help us with is when we hide them and pretend they don't exist. The secret place is no place for secrets. It's the place for total honesty and full disclosure. When we reveal our struggles, He releases the grace to help us change, lavishing us with acceptance, mercy, forgiveness and strength. This is how we let Him know who we really are. Many of us fear He might reject us if He really knew us; in reality, he accepts me when He sees the real me. *His acceptance is so incredible that it inspires me to open every single crevice of my heart to His loving eyes.* And this is where the intimacy is! The greatest intimacy is found in the mutual giving of ourselves radically to each other. It's the search for increasing self-disclosure that causes my relationship with Him to be deepened and enriched. When Jesus walked the Earth, He both knew the disciples implicitly *and* loved them unconditionally. This is the blessedness of being known by God!

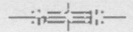

Prayer: *God of infinite love, I trust You explicitly. I have darkness in my heart, but I do not want to keep You out of my life. I want to be known by You and receive Your help as I continue on. I invite You again to search out the deep places of my heart—the hidden things, the weaknesses, the rebellion, even the things I don't recognize. As much as I want to know You, I also want to be known by You. And I believe that as I unveil myself to You, You will be faithful to forgive me and cleanse me from all unrighteousness, giving me the grace and strength I so desperately need. To be known by You is such a joyous privilege!*

Day 24 – The Secret of Intimacy First

Revelation 2:2-5

I know your works, your labor... and you have persevered and have patience, and have labored for My name's sake and have not become weary. Nevertheless I have this against you, that you have left your first love... repent and do the first works, or else I will come to you quickly and remove your lampstand from its place—unless you repent.

The first thing is the greatest thing: to love God with all your being. It's the greatest commandment (Matthew 22:37-38), and it's the first thing in our lives (Revelation 2:4). Intimacy with God must be our first priority before anything else, even our works of service. The second commandment (loving others, which are our works of service) "is like" the first commandment, according to Jesus, and yet Jesus clearly called it *second* (Matthew 22:39). It's an extremely close second and difficult to separate from the first at times, but it is definitely second.

It's vitally important that we keep first things first. When our love for God gets our first and best attention, then we will function in the spiritual wholeness necessary to execute the second commandment. When our priorities become inverted and we begin placing more emphasis on loving others than on loving God, we are headed for certain burnout. The only way to avoid an eventual collapse is to keep returning to our first love.

The Holy Spirit is profoundly committed to restoring the first commandment to first place in our lives. We must be established in our primary identity before God. It's so important to be able to say, "This is who I am. I am not primarily a worker for God; I am first and foremost a lover of God." The Holy Spirit's mandate is to establish our primary identity as lovers of God. *By the time He is finished in our lives, we will be lovers who work rather than workers who love.* And the responses of His heart will be lavishly explosive when we give Him our first and best energies.

Learn what it means to come to Him simply for the joy and delight of being with Him. He wants us addicted to the wine of His love (Song of Solomon 1:2), but it's so easy to become addicted to the wine of ministry. My first love used to be ministry; I was motivated more by what I did for God than by being with Him. What sustained me most was the "rush" of ministry accomplishments—and I didn't even realize it until the Lord showed it to me. It's not wrong to enjoy ministering to others, but it's so easy for this to become the addictive wine that intoxicates and fulfills us, all the while His love takes second place to this "new wine" we've tasted called ministry.

God wants us to be a people of "one thing (Luke 10:42)." There's only one thing that's really necessary: *the first commandment, the pursuit of a loving relationship with our dazzling Bridegroom.* The greatest dimensions of Kingdom power will be touched by those who are truly ignited and energized by their personal love relationship with the Lord Jesus.

Prayer: *Wise Father, I want to be a person of the "one necessary thing." I have neglected it for too long. I want that "good part which will not be taken away." I will love You first and derive my fulfillment and sense of success from the love You lavish on me in the secret place. Stabilize me by the power of an inner life with You. I don't want to be whipped around by the fluctuations of ministry or by my emotions. Set me ablaze with zeal for the face of Christ so that I may shine with the light of a relationship that enjoys intimacy first. Give me the simplicity and purity of devotion. Make the first command first place in my life! I want the secret place to be what I truly live for!*

Day 25 – The Secret of Bridal Identity

Revelation 22:17

And the Spirit and the Bride say, "Come!"

The bridal imagery of a cosmic wedding appears frequently throughout the entire Bible, starting in the beginning with Adam and Eve and ending with the last chapter of the Bible. The message is very clear and consistent: we are the Bride of Christ, being prepared for a great wedding celebration in the age to come, when we will be joined forever in great affection to our Bridegroom, the Lord Jesus Christ.

When Jesus looks at us, clothed in white garments of righteousness, replete with good works, mature in affections, making ourselves ready for our wedding day, His ravished heart soars with delight and desire for His espoused virgin, His Bride. He can hardly wait 'til that day—neither can we! In the meantime, we court each other with love, attention, words of affection, honor and delight. The secret place is the King's chamber (Song of Solomon 1:4), the place where we nurture our growing love relationship.

The secret place is not where we perform our sacred duty as a Believer but where we revel in the delight of being with the One our soul loves. This is where He speaks over us, declaring how beautiful and fair we are in His sight. We come primarily as His Bride, to enjoy His embrace and to lavish upon Him our love. *The secret place is a celebration of our highest identity—His Bride!* It's the place of intimate love exchange. We respond by opening our hearts to Him with greater abandonment, praising the glorious attributes of His beauty and character, and receiving the lavish affections of His heart. Oh, the exchange of love in the secret place is most glorious! He sure knows how to capture a heart and keep it!

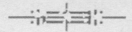

Prayer: *My amazing Bridegroom, show me Your love! I long to spend time with You and come to know You better. Your love is better than life—better than any good or great thing that this world can offer me. My soul cannot be entertained enough to make me happy; only being fascinated with You will truly satisfy my soul. Sometimes I lose focus on my identity as Your Bride, so I ask You to open my eyes to my true identity! Reveal Your love for me and consume my heart with bridal affection for You!*

Day 26 – The Secret of Clinging

Psalm 119:31

I cling to Your testimonies; oh Lord, do not put me to shame!

As "the weaker vessel," one of the things we feel deeply as the Bride of Christ is our helplessness and vulnerability apart from Him. Especially in times of difficulty or trouble, when we really feel our need for Him, we will cling to Him just as a person who can't swim might cling to a lifevest.

During crisis seasons, the secret place becomes our source of survival as we come aside to cling to Him and cry out for help. There are times when my soul is being blown about with winds, and I don't even understand the nature of the warfare. If I knew where the warfare was coming from, or if I knew how to defend myself, it would be a lot easier. But I'll find myself caught in a swirl of emotions and uncertainties, and I won't know what to do next. *The only thing I know to do in those times is to get away to the secret place, tremble before Him in my vulnerability, and cling to Him desperately.*

I used to think that Christian maturity meant that we got stronger and stronger until we were an intimidating force to be reckoned with by the powers of darkness. But the image of maturity that's given for us in Scripture is quite different from that: "Who is this coming up from the wilderness, leaning upon her beloved (Song of Solomon 8:5)?" Here we see the bride who has been perfected in love through the seasons of the wilderness, and what quality is most striking about her? She is depending upon her Beloved for help with every step! Experience has taught her that she needs Jesus' help in literally every area of her life, so she leans on Him and clings to Him with desperate dependence.

Prayer: *My strong, beloved God, I want to be so close to You! I am only granted a portion of Your nearness now, so I will cling to You in the secret place, and there I will give You my love. Be my strength for I am weak beyond what I will even admit. Even in this moment with You I am aware of my lack, but my spirit groans within me and my heart longs to be ever closer to You. Be near to me, my God—Your nearness is my good!*

Day 27 – The Secret of Walking with God

Hebrews 11:5

By faith Enoch was taken away so that he did not see death, "and was not found, because God had taken him"; for before he was taken he had this testimony, that he pleased God.

My wife, Marci, loves to go walking with her friend, Wendy. They talk the whole time. Nonstop. The walk not only makes exercise fun, it also deepens their friendship. Jesus went on these kinds of walks with His disciples, and He still likes to walk with us this way today. God created man for the enjoyment of a walking relationship that involves companionship, dialogue, intimacy, joint decision-making, mutual delight and shared communion.

The secret place is not the destination; it is only the catalyst. It is designed of God to establish us in an intimate friendship with Him that is walked out through the course of our everyday lives. *The goal we're after is an everyday walk of unbroken communion with our Lord and Friend.*

When the zeal of God captures you, it will ignite you with a great passion to walk with God and to be His friend. *When we walk with God, we enter the dimension where God unfolds the secrets of His Kingdom.* These are the paths that the ancients trod before us (Song of Solomon 1:7-8). Noah knew the secret of walking with God (Genesis 6:9), as did Abraham (Genesis 24:40). Through Christ, you can explore the glorious riches of knowing God like they did—and to an even greater degree because of the Spirit who has been given to us!

Jesus told us that He confides His Kingdom purposes to His friends (John 15:15). God wants to walk *with* us before He works *through* us. So He will wait to act until He finds the right man or woman through whom He can work. To put it bluntly, God works with His friends.

The secret place is where we develop a walking relationship with God. We must develop a secret history with God before He gives us a public ministry before people. Hidden in the secret place, we learn what He's looking for in friends, and we find out what pleases Him. Our inner chamber becomes our training ground for a life that is rooted and grounded in love.

Prayer: *My wonderful Friend, I want to be pulled into a closer walk with You. I want to feel what You feel and see my life the way You see it. I want to delight Your heart with my friendship. Let it be said of me that I pleased You because I walked with You all the days of my life. Capture me with the great secret of being Your friend!*

Day 28 – The Secret of Buying Oil

Matthew 25:1-13

Then the Kingdom of Heaven shall be likened to ten virgins who took their lamps and went out to meet the Bridegroom. Now five of them were wise, and five were foolish. Those who were foolish took their lamps and took no oil with them, but the wise took oil in their vessels with their lamps. But while the Bridegroom was delayed, they all slumbered and slept. And at midnight a cry was heard: "Behold, the Bridegroom is coming; go out to meet Him!" Then all those virgins arose and trimmed their lamps. And the foolish said to the wise, "Give us some of your oil, for our lamps are going out." But the wise answered, saying, "No, lest there should not be enough for us and you; but go rather to those who sell, and buy for yourselves." And while they went to buy, the Bridegroom came, and those who were ready went in with Him to the wedding; and the door was shut. Afterward the other virgins came also, saying, "Lord, Lord, open to us!" But He answered and said, "Assuredly, I say to you, I do not know you." Watch therefore, for you know neither the day nor the hour in which the Son of Man is coming.

Oil in the Bible is often representative of the Holy Spirit, so to have oil in our lamps means to have the indwelling presence of the Holy Spirit illuminating our lives with His zeal and glory. Without the oil of the Holy Spirit, our lives become lifeless, and our light is extinguished. The secret place is where we buy oil. As we come aside to commune with our Lord, we are renewed in the Holy Spirit and our oil level is replenished.

The idea of "buying oil" is derived from the parable of the ten virgins (Matthew 25:1-13). All ten virgins had oil in their lamps, but the five wise virgins brought an extra vessel of oil with them. This was because the wise virgins had anticipated that the return of the Bridegroom might possibly be delayed beyond their expectations. The foolish virgins made the fatal assumption that the Bridegroom's return would be sooner than later. They were confident that they didn't need extra oil; they thought their lamp held enough oil to sustain them until the Bridegroom's coming.

The oil could be said to represent a leader's ministry anointing that is cultivated in the secret place. The foolish virgins had a "get by" mentality. They invested themselves in the secret place only to the degree that their ministry responsibilities seemed to dictate. The wise showed their diligence by garnering a depth in God that was greater than their present ministry demanded of them. *The wise did not come to the secret place simply to buy oil for ministry; they also came to buy oil for themselves, in order to have a private burning-heart relationship with the Lord.* It doesn't cost much to get oil for ministry, but it will cost you a lot to get the oil of an intimate relationship with Jesus. Then, when the ministry time is over, you will still have a burning heart of love for Him. The oil of authentic relationship is bought at the cost of investing time and energy in the secret place.

When the Bridegroom delays His return, the virgins are overtaken with heartsickness because of deferred hope (Proverbs 13:12). Heartsickness will cause them to sleep from sorrow (Luke 22:45). The Bridegroom's delay has a way of distinguishing between the foolish and the wise. It reveals those who have developed their own personal history of a living relationship with the Bridegroom. The wise will understand that there are no shortcuts to ministry authority. *You can't derive the authority of anointing from another person or their teaching; you have to get it yourself in the secret place.* Those who persevere in love through the heartsickness of deferred hopes will be entrusted with the authority to minister deliverance to the captives; the wise will become mighty deliverers in the end.

Devote yourself to the secret place until your heart is overflowing with love and zeal for your Beloved. Then, make it the first priority of your day to keep that oil replenished. The secret is right here: *the secret place is the place of the replenishment you need to sustain you through the dark night of Christ's delays.* Buy oil!

———❧———

Prayer: *My departed Bridegroom, I want to be seen as wise by You. I come to You to be set ablaze by the fire of Your love. I believe You will come for me someday, but until then I will love You here and now. I do not come to You to gain a more influential ministry, I come to gain You alone. Renew my heart, Holy Spirit, so that I may pursue You with strong passion. Have mercy on me and see the intentions of my heart to gain oil. I do desire You, Father. Draw me closer to Yourself!*

Day 29 – The Secret of Abiding in Christ

John 15:7

If you abide in Me, and My words abide in you, you will ask what you desire, and it shall be done for you.

Throughout history, there has been a question asked by all of the great saints amidst their pursuit of God. It is the common quest of the diligent soul, the shared question of all generations, for all time. The question is very simply, "How do I abide in Christ?" The question is simple, but the answer profound. And few there be that find it.

Many of us feel like we move in and out of God's throneroom. We have times of great connectedness, and then we suffer periods of disconnectedness. We can't always analyze exactly why a distance has developed in our hearts toward the Lord, but most of us feel like our relationship with Christ is a roller coaster ride of feeling close, then far, then close, then far, then close again. And we hate it. We were created for constant intimacy, and anything less drives us crazy on the inside.

How you come to abide in Christ will be different from how anyone else does it. We all abide differently because we are all unique creations of God. Your relationship with Christ will never be like mine, and mine will never be like yours. That's why you'll never learn to abide by reading the right book or listening to a great sermon. A mentor might be able to help you to a degree, but in the final analysis, we all have to find our own way to abiding in Christ. *When all is said and done, we must shut the door, get into the secret place with God, and discover what an abiding relationship with Christ will look like for ourselves.*

Usually the pathway to an abiding relationship with Christ is attended with duress. God allows uncomfortable circumstances or emotions in our lives that press us into Christ with vigilant determination. Most of us will never abandon ourselves to pursuing an abiding relationship unless the Lord, in His kindness, allows calamities or struggles in our lives that elevate our pain level to the point of desperation. When you find this "river of life," this subterranean river that runs so deep that only a few find it, you will find a lifesource in God that goes deeper than the seasons of life. *Whether it's a flood season or a drought season, there is a river available to the saint providing a constant source of divine life and Spirit empowerment. Very few seem to find this great underground river, but when you find it, it is called "abiding in Christ."*

God has the same lesson for you that He gave to Joseph as he was thrown into a pit and then into a prison: what He's calling you to do will never be managed on the strength of your giftings and talents. And He knows that as long as your strengths are intact, you will always default to them. So He will put you in a place where your strengths will be useless—in prison! But the helplessness of losing all control will force you to find a dimension in the Lord that supercedes your giftings and talents. When Joseph found that river, it was his ability to draw upon the life of God that lifted him from the prison, not his talents. He interpreted Pharaoh's dream by tapping into the river of the Spirit and was moved from the prison to the palace in one day!

It is an abiding relationship with Christ that launches the saint into the dimension where God works sovereignly and mightily in the affairs of men. Do not be discouraged by the duress and hardship that has suddenly come upon you. It is an invitation from the Lord Himself! Press into God like you never have before and He will satisfy the longings of your heart to be closer to Him.

Prayer: *Sovereign Lord, cause my soul to be desperate for You so it will drive me to seek the abiding relationship that we both desire. Guide me to that ancient river that runs deep in Your heart, oh God. As I chase You with every ounce of strength I have, I ask that You take away all the abilities I rely on so I will fully lean upon You. Take away all that is easy so that I may gain You. However You deem wise, teach me to forever abide in You. I trust You, my faithful Father.*

Day 30 – The Secret of Union with God

John 17:24

Father, I desire that they also whom You gave Me may be with Me where I am, that they may behold My glory which You have given Me; for You loved Me before the foundation of the world.

There is a profound cry, deep within every human being for a heart connection with God. You were created to abide in Christ! It is this cry for intimacy with God that has driven you to read this book. It was that same cry for a connection with God that filled the heart of the Samaritan woman in John chapter four, even though she didn't know how to articulate her longings. She had looked for love in all the wrong places, but the Master saw her heart and knew how to draw it out. When the conversation was over, she found that above all else, the longing of her heart was for a meaningful connection with God Himself.

God has breathed into the human soul a profound desire for union with Him. Then He equipped us with the vocabulary to talk about it when He gave us the model of marriage. He said, "Therefore a man shall leave his father and mother and be joined to his wife, and they shall become one flesh (Genesis 2:24)." The union of marriage was to serve as an example that would give us a mental template for understanding spiritual union.

God has given us a great desire for union—with our spouse, and even moreso with Him. *We know there is a day coming in which we will be joined to Christ at the marriage supper of the Lamb, but Scripture has clearly shown that there are dimensions of union with Christ that are available to us in the here and now. The fullness is coming later, but what is available to us now is deserving of our diligent pursuit.*

But until then, I will retreat to my secret place, a heartsick, lovesick Bride who longs to behold her Bridegroom. I will pursue Him with the intent of overtaking Him. And I will exult in our quiet secret—the place of highest intimacy—for here I am joined to Him and we are one.

Prayer: *My passionate Bridegroom! You have created me for Yourself. My heart craves union with You; the unencumbered, overwhelming delight of being Yours and knowing that You are mine. In Your great grace, join our hearts together in eternal affections of love and devotion. Despite my weak will and my sin, my heart still aches to find that connection with You. Cause my love to be a constant, blessed torture to You so that You cannot help but reveal Yourself to me! And may the drawing power of Your desire for me energize me for the lifelong pursuit of encountering You! I love You, my God!*

About *The Children's Legacy*

The Children's Legacy is a non-profit 501(c)(3) ministry organization created to reach out to children in need. *The Children's Legacy* shares a wonderful working relationship with the *International House of Prayer* Missions Base in Kansas City, Missouri (IHOP-KC).

Currently, *The Children's Legacy* is seeking to secure a house which would serve as a children's home. The purpose of the home is to provide a family environment for children needing placement, but would become a permanent home for them if adoption is not possible.

The Children's Legacy also helps to support several overseas orphanage works. This support includes providing for children's workers and some of the basic needs of the children. If you are interested in obtaining more information or would like to support *The Children's Legacy*, we welcome you to visit our website at www.thechildrenslegacy.com, or fill out the form on the following page and send it to us.

☐ I want to partner with *The Children's Legacy* to give hope for the future and loving care to children in need.

> At this time I would like to give:
> ☐ $25 ☐ $50 ☐ $100 ☐ $1,000 Other $ _____

☐ I want to receive more info about IHOP-KC. I am specifically interested in_____

Please send all correspondence to:
The Children's Legacy
P.O. Box 480073
Kansas City, MO 64148

---

www.thechildrenslegacy.com

Name _____

Company _____

Title _____

Address _____

_____

City _____

State _____ Zip Code _____

Country _____

Phone _____

E-mail _____